Formerly
New Directions for
Mental Health Services

NEW DIRECTIONS FOR YOUTH DEVELOPMENT

Theory
Practice
Research

winter | 2001

Zero Tolerance:
Can Suspension and Expulsion Keep Schools Safe?

D1596117

Russell J. Skiba
Gil G. Noam　　*editors*

JOSSEY-BASS
A Wiley Company
www.josseybass.com

Zero Tolerance: Can Suspension and Expulsion Keep Schools Safe?
Russell J. Skiba, Gil G. Noam (eds.)
New Directions for Youth Development, No. 92, Winter 2001
Gil G. Noam, Editor-in-Chief

Microfilm copies of issues and articles are available in 16mm and 35mm, as well as microfiche in 105mm, through University Microfilms Inc., 300 North Zeeb Road, Ann Arbor, Michigan 48106-1346.

ISSN 1533-8916 (print)   ISSN 1537-5781 (online)   ISBN 0-7879-1441-X (print)

NEW DIRECTIONS FOR YOUTH DEVELOPMENT is part of The Jossey-Bass Psychology Series and is published quarterly by Wiley Subscription Services, Inc., a Wiley company, at Jossey-Bass, 989 Market Street, San Francisco, California 94103-1741. Periodicals postage paid at San Francisco, California, and at additional mailing offices. Postmaster: Send address changes to New Directions for Youth Development, Jossey-Bass, 989 Market Street, San Francisco, California 94103-1741.

SUBSCRIPTIONS cost $70.00 for individuals and $135.00 for institutions, agencies, and libraries. Prices subject to change. Refer to the order form at the back of this issue.

EDITORIAL CORRESPONDENCE should be sent to the Editor-in-Chief, Dr. Gil G. Noam, Harvard Graduate School of Education, Larsen Hall 601, Appian Way, Cambridge, MA 02138 or McLean Hospital, 115 Mill Street, Belmont, MA 02478.

Cover photograph by Getty Images.

Jossey-Bass Web address: www.josseybass.com

Manufactured in the United States of America on acid-free recycled paper containing 100 percent recovered waste paper, of which at least 20 percent is postconsumer waste.

Contents

Editors' Notes

WELCOME TO the first issue of New Directions for Youth Development!

This issue, *Zero Tolerance: Can Suspension and Expulsion Keep Schools Safe?*, grew directly out of a chance meeting between us when we were invited to present during the first hearings held by the U.S. Commission on Civil Rights Commission on Zero Tolerance. After listening to various panels comprising practitioners, policymakers, and youth advocates, it was our turn to address the effects of zero-tolerance policy from a research perspective. Commission members were surprised by the apparent lack of empirical research justifying this practice. It remains a troubling lesson that policy that affects the lives of so many youth can be introduced and maintained without any evidence of its effectiveness. When our panel finished, we had a chance to talk further and found that we share a commitment to prevention, safe learning environments, and positive youth development. We both believe in adequate structure and consequences for negative behavior, but not in the reflexive administration of punishment.

When Gil Noam became editor of this new journal, we decided to work on this first issue together and thereby expand our dialogue to include other authors and readers in an intensive focus on the issues inherent in zero tolerance. We sought authors nationally recognized for their work and leadership in research, policy, the law, and advocacy and whose broad experience and expertise allowed them to address the relevant issues at multiple levels. We brought together researchers and practitioners, prevention specialists and educators, and youth development experts who understand systems

NEW DIRECTIONS FOR YOUTH DEVELOPMENT, NO. 92, WINTER 2001 © WILEY PERIODICALS, INC.

and those who have created demonstration projects. We asked each set of authors to summarize one aspect of the complex puzzle that contributes to zero tolerance or its alternatives.

The chapters in this issue move from a consideration of the effectiveness of zero tolerance to an examination of alternatives. The first three chapters address the state of knowledge in research and the law concerning zero tolerance in general, as well as the broad issues of suspension and expulsion. The final three chapters move to an exploration of alternatives to zero tolerance—strategies that work in preventing school violence and connecting alienated youth—from the standpoint of general policy and specific model programs.

Zero tolerance has created an abundance of controversy through extension to "weapons" such as cough drops, nail files, and Tweety Bird chains. But although these incidents of trivial application have captured public attention, debates about zero tolerance and civil rights are fundamentally unsolvable in the political arena. For every critic of a particularly trivial application of zero tolerance, there will be an administrator or policymaker arguing that zero tolerance is a critical tool for preserving school discipline and school safety. The only way out of this quandary is to address the more fundamental educational questions: Does zero tolerance really work? Is it truly an effective tool for promoting school safety or improving student behavior? What are the most effective tools for preventing school violence? This issue addresses all of these questions in turn.

Major findings of this issue

A number of important themes emerge across the chapters that summarize the status of knowledge about zero tolerance as a school disciplinary policy:

• *Zero tolerance is a political, not an educational, solution.* Unlike many interventions for academic failure, zero tolerance was not developed through careful research or even the less formal but experiential knowledge of teachers and psychologists. Rather, zero tolerance as a school discipline philosophy developed in the political arena for political purposes. School districts and policymakers, faced with pressure to address violence in schools, expropriated wholesale a term from drug enforcement that provided at least the appearance of addressing the problem. Like many other politically popular solutions, however, the early implementation of zero tolerance paid little or no attention to whether the most expedient solution was also the most effective.

• *Practices and policies used for school discipline and school safety prevention must be evaluated as educational interventions.* The questions that zero tolerance poses can be researched readily: Are schools that use zero tolerance practices indeed safer than those that do not? Do such policies yield improved student behavior, lower rates of dropout, or improved test scores? The reviews of this practice from a broad range of researchers, practitioners, and prevention specialists lead to even more fundamental questions: Why has research on the effects of zero tolerance not been performed before now? To avoid ineffective and even negative effects, shouldn't any new disciplinary policy be pilot-tested before widespread adoption? Given a national educational context in which accountability has become a central tenet, shouldn't existing disciplinary and school violence-prevention strategies, including zero tolerance, be subject to rigorous evaluation to ensure they make a contribution to ensuring the safety of our children?

The data presented in the first three chapters in this issue make a strong case that whatever its appeal, zero tolerance has failed to demonstrate effectiveness in reducing school violence or improving student discipline. If anything, the school exclusions at the heart of zero-tolerance discipline appear to be discriminatory, ineffective, and probably incapable of positively affecting student outcomes, given what we know about schools and difficult students. The Bush administration's education agenda, No Child Left Behind, is noteworthy for its strong commitment to research-based practice, calling for the implementation of only those educational interventions that have been validated as effective through rigorous empirical evaluation. Given this criterion, one might well expect to see future opposition to zero tolerance by this administration, because a broad range of evaluation has failed to place that policy among the ranks of effective, research-based procedures.

• *There are alternatives to the use of zero tolerance that have been demonstrated as effective at both the national and the local programmatic levels.* Since 1997, no fewer than five panels have been convened or supported by the federal government that have extensively reviewed the literature on youth violence prevention in order to make recommendations concerning effective practice. Not one of these panels has designated zero tolerance as effective or even promising. Rather, those panels, like the distinguished authors in this issue, have found that addressing the problem of school violence requires going well beyond rhetoric to understanding the complexity of the personal and systemic factors that increase the probability of violence and designing interventions based on that understanding.

• *Effective strategies for violence prevention and school disciplinary improvement are comprehensive and instructionally based, and they are effective precisely because they seek to keep students included in their school community.* We did not ask chapter authors to adhere to any specific model of violence prevention in their recommendations concerning effective alternatives, so we found their consistency in recommending a trilevel model of prevention to be remarkable. Consistently, our best knowledge suggests that there is no single answer to the complex problems of school violence and school discipline. Rather, our efforts must address a variety of levels and include universal interventions that teach all students alternatives to violence, procedures to identify and reintegrate students who may be at risk for violence, and interventions specifically designed for students already exhibiting disruptive or aggressive behavior.

It is currently not typical in America's schools to use curricular approaches to teach students appropriate means of interaction and problem solving. Yet the programs and interventions with the best record of reducing youth violence are essentially instructional, teaching students methods for solving their personal and interpersonal problems without resorting to violence. Nor is it typical to struggle to keep the most problematic students in school: the advent of zero tolerance appears to have increased the use of suspension and expulsion, already the most prevalent disciplinary tools in America's public schools. Yet the chapter authors' examination of programs suggests that the most effective strategies in preventing school violence have a clear commitment to keeping students in. The data consistently show that the best, perhaps the only, way to solve the complex problems of violence and disruption in schools is not to put certain children out of sight or out of mind, but to make the commitment of time and resources necessary to help all children succeed.

Conclusion

It is improbable that any single educational strategy will be sufficient for dealing with the difficult issues of learning and discipline. Schools are highly complex environments in which a variety of risk factors from homes and communities, including violence, family conflict and instability, the effects of media violence, and peer pressure, all play a role. Regardless of their popularity or expediency, single-issue rhetorical solutions like zero tolerance will never be able to capture or respond to this complexity.

Rather, discipline that makes a positive contribution to school safety grows out of a deeper understanding of the factors that go into the estrangement and disengagement of children and youth from school, seeking to understand better the willingness of too many youth to become part of antisocial groups even when this activity puts them in grave danger and to address the inability on the part of many children and youth to foresee the consequences of violence. All children need schools that connect to social and mental health services and engage youth to participate in prosocial settings. The youth of this nation need smaller schools, so that all teachers and administrators really know each child, and individual advising that ensures that no child drops through the cracks.

Students who are at risk for violence need mentoring, after-school programs, and methods for learning to control and channel anger and aggression. Finally, effective schools need teachers who are supported and continuously trained so as to have the resources to make effective learning engaging for all students.

Within such a context, communicating and enforcing rules has an important place. Children need to learn how to shape their behavior within limits and consequences, and especially how to live and work together in society. The teaching and learning that come about through the application of rules and consequences is made more effective when placed in the context of teaching and learning about how to get along, how to be successful in school, and how to solve one's problems without resorting to aggression or violence.

We are under no illusion that the path to an alternative model of school discipline and school violence prevention is direct or easy. National educational policy is shaped by complex and competing forces, only one of which is documentation of effectiveness. Unfortunately, the model interventions and programs described in this issue may be closer to the ideal than the norm in American public education. The data presented here are, in a very real sense, educational history in progress—a record of past successes and failures in educational practice. In the long term, one can only hope that we can learn from the mistakes documented in the recent history of school discipline, so that we are not doomed to repeat them.

Russell J. Skiba
Gil G. Noam
Editors

Executive Summary

1. Zero tolerance, zero evidence: An analysis of school disciplinary practice

Russell J. Skiba, Kimberly Knesting

Despite the controversies that it has created in communities throughout the country, zero tolerance continues to be a widely used response to school disruption. This chapter explores the history, philosophy, and effectiveness of zero-tolerance school disciplinary strategies. It presents the following major findings:

- Although punishing both major and minor incidents is central to zero-tolerance philosophy, community and national reaction has grown as increasingly trivial incidents receive progressively harsher penalties.
- Although expulsion may be reserved for more serious incidents, school suspension is used for a wide range of misbehavior, including disruption, attendance-related issues, and noncompliance.
- Suspension and expulsion are used inconsistently across schools, often primarily as a function of classroom overreferral or poor school climate.
- Minority overrepresentation in suspension and expulsion has been documented for over twenty-five years. There is no evidence that this is explainable by either student poverty status or increased disruption on the part of minority students.

NEW DIRECTIONS FOR YOUTH DEVELOPMENT, NO. 92, WINTER 2001 © WILEY PERIODICALS, INC.

- A high rate of repeat offending indicates that school exclusion is not a particularly effective punishment. In the long term, suspension and expulsion are associated with an increased risk of school dropout and juvenile delinquency.

Emerging data indicate that preventive alternatives to school exclusion hold a great deal of promise for addressing school violence and disruption. Schools and school districts wishing to replace zero-tolerance policies with research-based policies and practices might begin by:

- Reserving zero-tolerance disciplinary removals for only the most serious and severe of disruptive behaviors and defining those behaviors explicitly.
- Replacing one-size-fits-all disciplinary strategies with graduated systems of discipline, with consequences geared to the seriousness of the infraction.
- Expanding the array of options available to schools for dealing with disruptive or violent behavior.
- Implementing preventive measures that can improve school climate and reconnect alienated students.
- Evaluating all school discipline or school violence-prevention strategies to ensure that those strategies are truly addressing student behavior and school safety.

2. School expulsion as a process and an event: Before and after effects on children at risk for school discipline

Gale M. Morrison, Suzanne Anthony, Meri H. Storino, Joanna J. Cheng, Michael J. Furlong, Richard L. Morrison

Schools face the complex challenge of meeting the educational and social needs of all children while maintaining safe and orderly campuses. An increasingly prevalent response to students who disrupt the learning environment is school expulsion. In examining expulsion as both a process and an event, the chapter authors arrived at these conclusions:

- A number of outcomes are possible following any recommendation to expel. Only about a third of reported weapons incidents actually lead to expulsion.
- The implementation of the Gun-Free Schools Act of 1994 has dramatically increased the prevalence of expulsion. Expulsion appears to be used more frequently in smaller, nonurban schools.
- Although a variety of behavioral pathways may lead to expulsion, one commonality appears to be poor school performance. The majority of expelled students do not appear to pose a threat of serious danger to the school environment.
- Students with disabilities appear to be overrepresented in school expulsion.
- Expellable offenses are often predictable in the light of a student's developmental history. Failure to consider this context limits the ability to develop effective consequences and interventions.
- School context contributes to the outcome of the expulsion process. School administrators with a broader view of child behavior appear to be capable of designing alternatives that reduce the use of school expulsion.
- Although little is known about the aftermath of school expulsion, being expelled seems to place students at risk for school failure and involvement with the juvenile justice system.
- The availability of alternative programs is inconsistent at best, and their effectiveness for the most part is unstudied.

Expulsion serves multiple purposes for events that have multiple causes. It is difficult to imagine that the expulsion process as now conceived could meet all needs in all circumstances. A number of recommendations flow from the understanding of expulsion as a process rather than an event:

- Replace zero-tolerance policies with a reasoned and appropriate approach to school discipline.

- Support and implement comprehensive prevention programs to enhance the protective nature of schools.
- Develop alternative discipline strategies to replace school expulsion, and offer educational options when expulsion is necessary.
- Develop clear policies and procedures for the administration of school expulsion, and increase the accuracy of reporting procedures.
- Encourage and expand research interest on the practice and impact of school expulsion.

3. Zero tolerance: Unfair, with little recourse

Judith A. Browne, Daniel J. Losen, Johanna Wald

This chapter examines racial disparities in the application of zero tolerance and harsh disciplinary codes in our nation's public schools and the impact of these on minority children. It describes the legal avenues available to parents and children's advocates interested in challenging these policies and summarizes recent court decisions issued on zero tolerance and other school discipline cases. The authors find:

- National-level data show that in 1998–1999, African American students, about 17 percent of all students, accounted for 33 percent of all those suspended and 31 percent of all those expelled.
- State and local data reflect these same racial disparities in discipline. In some states with relatively few African American students, the rate of discipline is approximately three to four times greater than their proportion in the general student body.
- State-level data from South Carolina reflect the findings of national reports that African American students appear to be punished more severely than white students for minor or more subjective infractions.
- African American and other minority students may perceive these disparities as a sign of rejection by the system, contributing to their increased misbehavior or school dropout.

In response, parents and advocates have pursued a number of legal avenues, challenging exclusionary policies in court, including these:

- Protections against discrimination on the basis of color or national origin through the equal protection clause of the Fourteenth Amendment to the U.S. Constitution and enforcement efforts of the Office for Civil Rights under Title VI of the Civil Rights Act of 1964
- Challenges of zero-tolerance policies under the First Amendment, although First Amendment protections afforded students are not as expansive as those that are extended outside educational settings
- Procedural and substantive due process protections under the Fourteenth Amendment, although such challenges have met with mixed results
- Protections afforded students with disabilities under the Individuals with Disabilities Education Act, based on the rights of students with disabilities to a free and appropriate public education
- The fundamental right to a public education guaranteed by many state constitutions.

The success of some parent and advocacy groups in bringing about changes in disciplinary policy suggests that although strategic legal action remains an important avenue for parents and advocates to pursue, they might be well advised to do so in concert with other public education, lobbying, and organizing efforts.

4. Alternative strategies for school violence prevention

Joseph C. Gagnon, Peter E. Leone

This chapter reviews the efficacy of programming in three areas: universal or schoolwide approaches, targeted or intensive interventions for individual students or groups of students, and the use of security measures such as metal detectors and surveillance cameras. Within this framework, a number of programs with empirical evidence of effectiveness in addressing problems of aggression and disruption have emerged, including these:

- The Resolving Conflict Creatively Program, a social-cognitive intervention in which students are taught conflict resolution through modeling, role playing, interviewing, and small group work
- Project ACHIEVE, a universal intervention for elementary and middle schools that trains school personnel in effective methods of teaching social competence, effective instruction, and organizational planning
- Positive Behavior Interventions and Supports, a team-based model that seeks to restructure school-based discipline, including a common approach to discipline, positive expectations, and a continuum of procedures for rule violation
- Early detection through schoolwide procedures, such as the Systematic Screening of Behavioral Disorders, and early identification of students experiencing difficulty
- The Positive Adolescent Choices Training program, a cognitive-behavioral intervention designed to address the cultural needs of adolescent African American students at risk for violence
- The First Step to Success program, a student-centered approach designed for students in kindergarten exhibiting aggressive or defiant behavior
- Intensive interventions, such as functional behavioral assessment or alternative schools, that provide support for students who do not benefit from universal interventions or those that target small groups of students.

Although many schools have turned to school security technology or personnel to address safety concerns, data documenting the effectiveness of school security measures are both less extensive and less promising than for universal or student-centered approaches.

Schools that effectively prevent serious misconduct have policies, practices, and routines that support the implementation of research-validated practices. Following are specific recommendations:

- The presence of clear rules and consequences
- Administrative support that is visible, predictable, and continuous
- Ongoing support and consultation for staff
- Parent and community involvement across settings in implementing prevention programs
- Needs assessment and functional assessment to identify local needs
- Staff investment and comprehensive staff training
- Conflict resolution and social skills training for students
- Program monitoring and effective implementation.

5. The best approach to safety is to fix schools and support children and staff

David M. Osher, Susan Sandler, Cameron Lynn Nelson

Zero tolerance presumes that removing some students is necessary for school safety. In contrast, two national reports find that school commitment to maintaining all students in school and ensuring the success of those students can make the school safer for all students. Both investigations are consistent in finding:

- Safe schools provide all students with the supports and skills they need to develop appropriate behaviors and healthy emotional adjustment.
- Schools that are most successful establish a caring culture that provides a sense of belonging for students and helps them identify with the school community.
- Successful schools address challenges of disconnectedness by building a school community grounded in the culture, knowledge, and interests of diverse students.
- Schools committed to the success of all students intervene quickly when students, staff, or families are having problems.

- Staff are aware of early warning signs and apply such signs not to label but to help.
- When problems are identified, successful schools respond in a manner that is sensitive, strengths based, and individualized.
- Schools committed to serving all students employ intensive and individualized interventions to enable their more troubled students to succeed.
- Individualized and culturally competent school-based mental health services are provided.
- Interventions, including temporary exclusion from the classroom, are based on problem solving and continued membership in the school community.
- A team-based approach is used to respond to serious incidents of disruption.
- Alternative settings emphasize a positive environment, instruction in alternative behaviors, and a quick return to the mainstream.
- These comprehensive and meticulous approaches are supported by thoughtful attention to issues of staff deployment and time, school size, and the quality of leadership.

Policymakers at all levels of government can implement this approach through a variety of actions:

- Provide tools and incentives to schools to develop a shared mission.
- Support the development of small schools and schools within schools.
- Provide professional development and support opportunities.
- Provide time and financial resources for staff to develop and implement programs to support mission and programs in the areas of a schoolwide foundation, early intervention, and intensive intervention.

The schools studied in these reports explode the myth that it is necessary to choose between harsh discipline and safe and productive schools. They demonstrate that it is possible to create schools that are humane, caring places where discipline issues are minimized and become opportunities for growth and development. Equally important, these schools demonstrate that it is possible to turn around schools with significant discipline problems.

6. Beyond the rhetoric of zero tolerance: Long-term solutions for at-risk youth

Gil G. Noam, Laura A. Warner, Leigh Van Dyken

This chapter proposes an alternative to zero-tolerance policies without compromising school safety. The RALLY program (Responsive Advocacy for Life and Learning in Youth), dealing with high-risk youth, is an in-school prevention and intervention program combining mental health and educational practice to support students' progress both in and outside the classroom. The program:

- Aims to foster resiliency through relationship building while working toward academic success and socioemotional development.
- Introduces a new role of prevention practitioners, who work to address the needs of all students in their classrooms, whether they are considered at risk or not.
- Pulls services into the child's educational environment, in contrast to traditional case management, in which a child is pulled out of the classroom context to receive services, thus decreasing stigma and making these services available to all children.
- Uses a three-tiered approach to prevention in the classroom: inclusive prevention, targeted prevention, and high intensity prevention and intervention.

When schools become places in which students wish to learn instead of institutions of estrangement and marginalization, the overall safety of schools and the quality of education will increase. Connecting the worlds of children and providing early detection of educational, social, and mental health issues increases the chances of affecting the root causes of the behaviors that zero tolerance seeks to curb.

Russell J. Skiba
Gil G. Noam
Editors

Because there is little or no evidence of the efficacy of zero tolerance, schools and school districts need to explore preventive alternatives.

1

Zero tolerance, zero evidence: An analysis of school disciplinary practice

Russell J. Skiba, Kimberly Knesting

IN FORT MYERS, Florida, an eighteen-year-old senior and National Merit Scholar spent a day in jail, was suspended for five days, and missed graduation after a kitchen knife was found in the back seat of her car. In Deer Lakes, Pennsylvania, a five year old was suspended for wearing a five-inch plastic ax as part of his firefighter's costume to a Halloween party in his classroom. In Fairborn, Ohio, a fourteen year old was threatened with expulsion for sharing over-the-counter analgesic tablets with a classmate. In Glendale, Arizona, a seventh grader was suspended for four months for violation of weapons policy when, inspired by the movie *October Sky*, he brought a homemade rocket made from a potato chip canister to school. In Chicago, a high school junior who shot a paper clip with a rubber band and hit a cafeteria worker instead of the friend he was aiming at was expelled, taken to county jail for seven hours, and encouraged to drop out of school.

Cases such as these, reported in the national media, have created an intense national controversy about the practice of zero-tolerance school discipline. In the wake of Columbine and other

NEW DIRECTIONS FOR YOUTH DEVELOPMENT, NO. 92, WINTER 2001 © WILEY PERIODICALS, INC.

shootings, there can be no doubt that schools and school boards have the right, indeed the responsibility, to take strong action to preserve the safety of students, staff, and parents on school grounds. Yet critics of such harsh punishments claim that these incidents show a lack of common sense in punishment and raise questions of fairness and the extent to which extreme consequences truly contribute to either school safety or the improvement of student behavior.

These divided reactions reflect the profound ambivalence inherent in school disciplinary practice since the early 1990s. Ensconced as federal policy, at least one component of a zero-tolerance approach is currently in place in over 80 percent of the nation's schools. Each new outbreak of violence seems to yield a collateral increase in get-tough discipline. In turn, each new cycle of tougher policy—increased use of school security measures and a dramatic surge in school suspensions and expulsions—yields a new round of controversy and charges of civil rights violations.

This chapter explores the history and ever expanding use of zero tolerance in schools. In an analysis of a representative sampling of zero-tolerance suspensions and expulsions, we seek to provide insight into the practice and controversy of zero tolerance. We would argue that as striking as these nationally publicized incidents are, they are less important than the outcomes of zero-tolerance policy. Thus, the heart of this investigation is a consideration of research on the effects and side effects of current disciplinary practices in the schools. How well do strategies associated with zero tolerance appear to work in changing students' behavior or guaranteeing the safety of schools?

History, definition, and prevalence of zero tolerance

Zero tolerance first received national attention as the title of a program developed in 1986 by Peter Nunez, the U.S. attorney in San Diego, impounding seagoing vessels carrying any amount of drugs. U.S. Attorney General Edwin Meese highlighted the program as a national model in 1988, and he ordered customs officials to seize the vehicles and property of anyone crossing the border with even trace amounts of drugs and charge those individuals in federal court. The language of zero tolerance seemed to fire the public imagination; within months, the term and strategy began to be applied to a broad range of issues, from environmental pollution and trespassing to skateboarding, homelessness, and boom boxes.

Frightened by a seemingly overwhelming tide of violence, educators in the early 1990s were eager for a no-nonsense response to drugs, gangs, and weapons. Beginning in 1989, school districts in California, New York, and Kentucky picked up on the term *zero tolerance* and mandated expulsion for drugs, fighting, and gang-related activity. By 1993, zero-tolerance policies had been adopted across the country, often broadened to include not only drugs and weapons but also smoking and school disruption.

This tide swept zero tolerance into national policy when the Clinton administration signed the Gun-Free Schools Act of 1994 into law. The law mandates a one-year calendar expulsion for possession of a firearm, referral of law-violating students to the criminal or juvenile justice system, and the provision that state law must authorize the chief administrative officer of each local school district to modify such expulsions on a case-by-case basis. Originally, the bill covered only firearms, but more recent amendments have broadened the language of the act to include any instrument that may be used as a weapon.

State legislatures and local school districts have broadened the mandate of zero tolerance beyond the federal mandates of weapons, to drugs and alcohol, fighting, threats, and swearing.[1] Many school boards continue to toughen their disciplinary policies; some have begun to experiment with permanent expulsion from the system for some offenses. Others have begun to apply school suspensions, expulsions, or transfers to behaviors that occur outside school.

Since the passage of the Gun-Free Schools Act, some form of zero-tolerance policy appears to have become prevalent in public schools. Defining zero tolerance as a policy that mandates predetermined consequences or punishments for specified offenses, the National Center on Education Statistics (NCES) report, *Violence in America's Public Schools: 1996–1997*,[2] found that 94 percent of all schools have zero-tolerance policies for weapons or firearms, 87 percent for alcohol, and 79 percent for violence or tobacco.

It is important to note that the NCES definition of zero tolerance is quite broad. Undoubtedly, there are few school disciplinary policies that do not mandate some predetermined consequences for specific behaviors, and it is possible that an overly broad definition is responsible for the high prevalence rates reported for zero tolerance in the NCES study. A more typical, and more limited, definition of *zero tolerance* is as a disciplinary policy that is "intended primarily as a method of sending a message that certain behaviors will not be tolerated, by punishing all offenses severely, no matter how minor."[3]

Indeed, swift and certain consequences for all incidents, major or minor, seem to be at the heart of the zero-tolerance philosophy. In a 1982 article in *Atlantic Monthly*, George Kelling and William Wilson outline what they called broken-window theory, arguing that there is a relationship in high-crime neighborhoods between seemingly minor phenomena, such as broken windows, and more serious violent crime. The implication for crime prevention is that relatively minor incidents that signal disruption or violence cannot be ignored because "untended behavior leads to a breakdown of community control."[4]

Zero-tolerance punishments, targeting both serious and less serious behaviors, are thus meant to send a clear message to potential troublemakers that certain behaviors will not be tolerated. Charles Ewing, a professor of law and psychology, argues that zero tolerance "appropriately denounces violent student behavior in no uncertain terms and serves as a deterrent to such behavior in the future by sending a clear message that acts which physically harm or endanger others will not be permitted at school under any circumstances."[5] Proponents of zero tolerance argue that in the context of what appears to be a near epidemic of school violence, severe and certain consequences have a deterrent value that may make disruptive or violent students think hard before engaging in acts of aggression or disruption.

It is difficult to argue with the philosophy of zero tolerance. Recent school safety surveys have continued to find that minor disruption and serious violence in schools are to some extent related.[6] Thus, it makes eminent sense to attempt to address day-to-day disruption in an attempt to prevent more serious problems. Certainly, there are not many educators or parents who would wish to send any message other than one of nonacceptance for guns, weapons, or drugs in school settings.

Yet somewhere between the original philosophy of zero tolerance and its current widespread implementation in schools, the situation has become vastly more complicated. Applications of zero tolerance have led to lawsuits by parents, scathing editorials, and even hearings before the U.S. Commission on Civil Rights.[7] Thus, it seems appropriate to examine the actual practice of zero tolerance. How has it been used? What are the controversies it has created? How effective has it been in creating safer schools and more civil behavior among students?

The controversy of zero tolerance

Controversy has attended a host of suspensions and expulsions associated with zero tolerance for relatively trivial incidents in school settings almost from the inception of those policies. In a previous analysis, Skiba and Peterson catalogued some of the incidents that received media attention from the passage of the Gun-Free Schools Act in 1994 until May 1998, including school suspensions and expulsions for reasons ranging from possession of a fingernail file to offering a friend an organic cough drop. This chapter updates that analysis by examining cases of suspension or expulsion due to zero tolerance reported in national newspapers from May 1998 to May 2001.[8]

Weapons

Many accounts of zero tolerance tend to presume that the Gun-
Free Schools Act of 1994 is the driving force of local zero-tolerance efforts. Yet just as state and local zero-tolerance policies
predated federal law in this area, the following examples suggest
that local practice often extends zero tolerance considerably beyond
federal mandates:[9]

• October 1999, Atlanta, Georgia: A fifteen-year-old South
Cobb High School sophomore found with an unloaded gun in his
book bag was permanently expelled from the school district. The
youth was also charged in juvenile court with possession of a
weapon.

• September 1998, Seattle, Washington: A sixth grader at Whitman Middle School was expelled when a squirt gun, painted black
and brown, fell out of his backpack in the lunchroom. Although the
expulsion was upheld by a hearing officer, the Seattle School District reduced the expulsion to a suspension after the family's attorney cited state law requiring districts to provide a lesser punishment
where toy weapons were not used with malice or in a threatening
manner.

• September 2000, Atlanta, Georgia: Eleven-year-old Ashley
Smith was suspended for two weeks from Garrett Middle School
for possession of a ten-inch novelty chain attaching her Tweety
Bird wallet to her key ring. School officials stated that district policy was clear, classifying a chain as a weapon, in the same category
as pellet guns, ice picks, and swords.

• March 2001, Irvington, New Jersey: Two second graders were
suspended and charged by local juvenile authorities with making
terroristic threats after pointing a piece of paper folded to look like
a gun at classmates and saying, "I'm going to kill you all." The
superintendent of the district noted, "I thought this was very unfortunate. But, being that kids are being shot in schools across the
country, children have to be taught they can't say certain words in
public." The father of one of the boys disagreed, stating, "This is
just stupid, stupid, stupid. How can you take two boys to the police
precinct over a paper gun? This is very bad judgment."

These incidents underscore two sources of controversy inherent in zero-tolerance incidents. In the first incident, involving a shotgun in a backpack, there can be little doubt of the seriousness of the offense; in this case, however, it is not the necessity of the expulsion but rather its length that makes the incident newsworthy. Other incidents appear to cause controversy by defining as a weapon an object, such as a chain attached to a Tweety Bird wallet, that poses little real danger. Yet this apparent overextension is consistent with the philosophical intent of zero tolerance, treating both major and minor incidents with severity in order to set an example. Indeed, the apparent lengthening of expulsions over time may be related to the use of harsh punishment for less severe offenses. If a student is suspended or expelled for an object (such as a squirt gun or folded paper) that is a weapon only through interpretation, districts may feel a need to distinguish truly dangerous incidents by extending punishment even further for actual weapons.

Drugs

Although there is no federal mandate of suspension or expulsion for drug-related offenses, the application of zero tolerance to drugs or alcohol has become quite common, with the gravity of the events varying considerably:[10]

- June 1998, Brookline, Massachusetts: Nine seniors caught with alcohol on a bus going to their senior prom were barred from attending their graduation, and two were not allowed to compete in the state baseball playoffs. Citing tragic accidents caused by alcohol abuse, the school headmaster stated, "It's important for kids to get the message that if they do something that violates some of the fundamental rules we have here, they will be punished."
- October 1998, East Lake, Florida: High school senior Jennifer Coonce took a sip of sangria at a luncheon with coworkers as part of a school-sponsored internship. When her parents called the high school to complain about minors being served alcohol, the district suspended her for the remainder of the semester. Jennifer, an honors student, was offered the opportunity to take her college placement classes at home, over the telephone.

• December 2000, Casco, Maine: A fifteen-year-old high school student who took pills given to her by classmates for a headache was expelled for violation of the district's zero-tolerance antidrug policy. The student who gave the girl the pills was also expelled by the school board.

The range of seriousness of these incidents, as compared with the relative consistency of punishment, may offer some insight into why zero tolerance creates controversy. A fairly stiff punishment for serious drinking or drug abuse at school-sponsored events seems fitting and may well serve to prevent more serious harm. In contrast, the long-term suspension of an honors student for a sip of sangria seems more likely to turn the offender into the perceived victim.

Strictures against cruel and unusual punishment are fundamental to the U.S. legal system. It may well be that school punishments greatly out of proportion to the offense arouse controversy by violating basic perceptions of fairness inherent in our system of law, even when upheld by the courts.

Threats

Incidents of lethal school violence, and the copy-cat threats those incidents appear to have spawned, have made school personnel especially sensitive to threats of violence in school. It is not surprising that zero tolerance has been the strategy that some schools and districts have chosen to address threats. Incidents reported in national newspapers since May 1998 include the following:[11]

• March 2001, Topeka, Kansas: At Wabaunsee High School, a fifteen-year-old student wrote a message that he was going to "get you all" on the boys' bathroom wall. After school personnel erased the message, he wrote a second message stating that he should be taken seriously and was "going to shoot everyone." The boy, arrested and charged with one count of criminal threat, returned to school after a five-day suspension. Some parents protested the leniency of the school punishment. "I know kids who have been suspended for three days just for orneriness and this kid threatened to kill the whole student body," complained one parent.

• November 1999, Ponder, Texas: When a thirteen year old wrote a Halloween story for class that involved getting high on Freon, opening fire on a suspected intruder, and finally shooting his teacher and several classmates, the boy was ordered held in a juvenile detention facility for ten days. The Denton County district attorney noted that the decision to hold him was based on a review of records indicating that the boy had been "a persistent discipline problem for this school, and the administrators there were legitimately concerned."

• March 2001, Burbank, Illinois: After a band concert, a junior at Reavis High School in this Chicago suburb and three friends put together a list of twenty members of fellow band members they did not like. When rumors spread that the list was really a "hit list," the student, acknowledged as an active and bright student, was suspended for four days and kicked out of band. "It's crazy," stated the boy's mother, herself an assistant principal at a Chicago high school. "There's a difference between saying 'I'm going to come to school with a gun and blow everybody up,' and saying, 'Here are kids who annoy me.'"

Recent school shooting incidents provide an unequivocal lesson that schools may place themselves at risk by ignoring serious threats of violence. It is not surprising, then, to see an increase in zero-tolerance incidents regarding threat in the aftermath of an incident such as the Santana High School shooting in early March 2001. Indeed, some reactions to threat may be perceived by the community as too lenient, as in the threat at Waubansee High School.

Yet the local and in some cases national furor created by some of these incidents suggests that there may be limits on what a school can or should do to protect staff and students. Indeed, automatic school exclusion for threats of violence is unlikely to solve the complex problems of threatened violence in schools. In its report *The School Shooter: A Threat Assessment Perspective*, the FBI issued a strong caution:

It is especially important that a school not deal with threats by simply kicking the problem out the door. Expelling or suspending a student for making a threat must not be a substitute for careful threat assessment and a considered, consistent policy of intervention. Disciplinary action alone, unaccompanied by any effort to evaluate the threat or the student's intent, may actually exacerbate the danger—for example if a student feels unfairly or arbitrarily treated and becomes even angrier and more bent on carrying out a violent act.[12]

The report recommends instead that schools conduct a careful four-pronged assessment to determine the seriousness of any threat, and develop a team approach to threat evaluation and intervention.

What the zero-tolerance incidents tell us

There is some tendency to assume that these suspensions or expulsions for trivial incidents are simply idiosyncratic or silly aberrations that occur in districts characterized by an overzealous administration. Yet the ubiquity of these apparently trivial incidents across time and location suggests that the overextension of school sanctions to minor misbehavior is not anomalous but rather inherent in the philosophy and application of zero tolerance. National and local data suggest that truly dangerous behavior occurs relatively infrequently in schools and that the most frequent disciplinary events with which schools wrestle are minor disruptive behaviors such as tardiness, class absence, disrespect, and noncompliance.[13] Targeting both minor and major disciplinary events equally will, almost by definition, result in the punishment of a small percentage of serious infractions and a much larger percentage of relatively minor misbehavior. We might expect that the minor incidents connected with zero tolerance will not abate, and may even accelerate, as those policies continue to be extended by local districts.

The number of lawsuits filed by parents in response to such incidents also appears to be increasing. In general, courts have tended to side with school districts in reviewing such cases, giving relatively broad leeway to district administrators in their interpretation of school disciplinary policy. Yet the courts have also begun to limit school district power in certain cases if the policy appears to violate district or state law or fails to provide due process protections.[14]

Administrators in these high-profile incidents often claim that they have little or no room for flexibility in the administration of district policy. Yet this intractability represents a local interpretation of zero tolerance that may go beyond the spirit of federal zero-tolerance policy. Indeed, by requiring local districts to have in place a procedure allowing for case-by-case review, the Gun-Free Schools Act seems to mandate some degree of flexibility in the implementation of zero tolerance.

Reaction to these events leaves communities highly divided. Proponents argue that increased flexibility in the administration of consequences will send a message to potential violators that schools are not serious about enforcement. Parents and student advocates have countered that when the punishment fails to fit the crime, students are learning nothing about justice and much about what they must do to subvert rules and policies. This sometimes emotional debate seems almost irreconcilable, pitting school safety against student civil rights.

Yet a more fundamental and important question concerns the outcomes and effectiveness of zero tolerance. If zero tolerance can be shown to be a key component in maintaining safe schools and civil student behavior, then schools might well consider limits on student civil rights to be justified in some instances. But if zero tolerance has not been shown to be effective, then the use of a procedure with such harsh side effects for individual students hardly seems justified.

It has been more than ten years since school districts began adopting zero-tolerance policies and over five years since the strategy was made national policy by the Gun-Free Schools Act. Given the current climate of educational accountability, one would expect some data to have emerged concerning the effects and effectiveness of zero-tolerance approaches. To what extent have the disciplinary practices associated with zero tolerance led to increased school safety or improved student behavior?

Effects and effectiveness of zero tolerance: Suspension and expulsion

The use of school exclusion, that is, suspension and expulsion, might be regarded as the central feature of zero-tolerance policy: one-year expulsions are written into federal and state regulations regarding zero tolerance. Six years after the implementation of the Gun-Free Schools Act, there is surprisingly little national-level data available on trends concerning the use of suspension and expulsion over time. Yet some state and local data suggest that applications of zero tolerance have dramatically increased the use of school suspension and expulsion in at least some school districts (see also Chapters Two and Three in this issue).

How suspension and expulsion are used

One would expect that suspension and expulsion, as more severe consequences, would tend to be reserved for more serious infractions. Yet zero-tolerance policies seeking to punish all behaviors severely may to some extent erase the notion of a graduated set of consequences geared to the severity of behavior. How frequently are suspension and expulsion used, and in response to what behaviors? Available data suggest a different pattern of use for school suspension and school expulsion.

Expulsion appears to be reserved for incidents of moderate to high severity, although not always for those students who are most troublesome or dangerous (see Chapter Two). Suspension, in contrast, is among the most widely used disciplinary techniques. In one midwestern city, one-third of all office referrals resulted in a one- to five-day suspension, and 21 percent of all enrolled students were suspended at least once during the school year. Suspension appears to be used with greater frequency in urban areas than in suburban or rural areas.[15]

As might be expected with such high rates, school suspension is not always reserved for serious or dangerous behaviors. Fights or other physical aggression among students are consistently found to be among the most common reasons for suspension. Yet school suspension is also commonly used for a number of relatively minor offenses, such as disobedience and disrespect, attendance problems, and general classroom disruption. In fact, students are suspended for the most serious offenses (drugs, weapons, vandalism, assaults on teachers) relatively infrequently.[16]

Consistency and fairness of school discipline

Commonsense notions of justice demand that punishments in school or society be administered fairly and consistently. Although it is not unreasonable that discipline policies vary from school to school, it is reasonable to expect that student behavior, rather than idiosyncratic characteristics of schools or classrooms, will be the primary determinant of school punishment.

There can be little doubt that certain students are at a much greater risk for office referral and school suspension. One national study found that students who were suspended were more likely to endorse statements indicating an antisocial attitude. Students who engage in harassment, bullying, or violent behavior appear to be at greater risk of future disciplinary action. Some students clearly account for a disproportionate share of disciplinary effort; in one study in nineteen middle schools in a large midwestern urban district, 6 percent of students were responsible for 44 percent of all referrals to the office.[17]

Individual difference and family characteristics appear to be likely correlates with involvement in school discipline processes. Students with substantiated reports of abuse or neglect are significantly more likely to be referred for school discipline and somewhat more likely to be suspended, especially at the middle and high school levels. One study reported that of students who were suspended, 43 percent at the high school level and 38 percent at the middle school level showed evidence of an emotional or behavioral disorder on one or more student *and* teacher subscales of the Child Behavior Checklist.[18]

Yet school disciplinary actions cannot be accounted for solely in terms of student behaviors; they are also a function of classroom and school characteristics. In one middle school, two-thirds of all disciplinary referrals came from 25 percent of the school's teachers. School factors also strongly influence rates of suspension. Comparisons of schools with high and low use of school suspension indicate that low-suspension schools spend less time on discipline-related matters, have a lower student-teacher ratio and a higher level of academic quality, and pay significantly better attention to issues of school climate. Indeed, in multivariate analyses of factors predicting suspension, school characteristics, such as overall suspension rate, teacher attitudes, administrative centralization, quality of school governance, teacher perception of student achievement, and racial makeup of the school, appear to be more strongly predictive of school suspension than student attitudes and behavior.[19]

Racial fairness in school punishments

The expulsion of seven African American students for two years by the Decatur Public Schools for a football game brawl, and the subsequent suit brought by the Reverend Jesse Jackson and Operation PUSH on behalf of those students, represents the most publicized incident to date involving racial disproportionality in school discipline. Yet minority overrepresentation in school punishments is not a new issue. Both racial and economic biases in school suspension and expulsion have been studied extensively for over twenty-five years, with highly consistent results.

Disproportionality due to socioeconomic status. Studies of school suspension have consistently documented overrepresentation of low-income students in the use of that consequence. Field studies have found that both high- and low-income adolescents feel that disciplinary practices are unfairly weighted against poor students. Whereas high-income students were more likely to receive mild and moderate consequences (such as a lecture by the teacher or moving their desk in the classroom), low-income students reported receiving more severe consequences, sometimes delivered in a less-than-professional manner (for example, they were yelled at in front of the rest of the class, made to stand in the hall all day, or had their personal belongings searched).[20]

Racial disproportionality in discipline. Racial disproportionality in the use of school suspension has been a highly consistent finding (see also Chapter Three).[21] Black students are also exposed more frequently to more punitive disciplinary strategies, such as corporal punishment, and receive fewer mild disciplinary sanctions when referred for an infraction.[22] In the most recent study of racial disproportionality in discipline, the Applied Research Center of Oakland, California, reported higher-than-expected rates of suspension and expulsion for black students in all fifteen major U.S. cities studied.

One possible explanation is that overuse of suspension for black students is not necessarily racial bias but rather a corollary of the documented disproportionality in discipline for students from lower socioeconomic backgrounds. Yet race appears to make a contribution to disciplinary outcome independent of socioeconomic status. Multivariate analyses have found that even when socioeconomic status is statistically controlled, race still makes a significant contribution to who gets suspended.[23]

It is also possible that the higher rates of school exclusion and punishment are due to correspondingly high rates of disruptive behavior. In such a case, disproportionality would represent not racial bias but a relatively appropriate response to disproportionate misbehavior. Yet investigations of student behavior, race, and discipline have found no evidence that African Americans misbehave at a significantly higher rate.[24] If anything, available research suggests that black students tend to receive harsher punishments than white students and that those harsher consequences may be administered for less severe offenses. In a report entitled *The Color of Discipline*, researchers at the Indiana Education Policy Center found no evidence that African American students engaged in more serious misbehavior; rather, black students were referred to the office more than white students for more judgmental reasons, including loitering, disrespect, and excessive noise.[25] Thus, far from engaging in higher levels of disruptive behavior, African American students may be at risk for receiving a range of more severe consequences for less serious behavior.

Effectiveness of suspension and expulsion

In 1999, the U.S. Department of Education released its *Report on State Implementation of the Gun-Free Schools Act: School Year 1997–98.*[26] The report focused on expulsions of students in fifty states and territories for bringing a weapon to school (the report did not include data on expulsions of students for offenses other than weapons). Of the 3,390 weapons-related expulsions reported for the school year, 61 percent were for handguns, 7 percent for rifles, and 32 percent for "other firearms." The majority of reported expulsions (57 percent) occurred at the high school level. The number of reported expulsions for weapons showed an apparent decrease, from 5,724 in 1996–97 to 3,930 in 1997–98. The report cautions that the decrease may be due to differences in reporting across the two years but also suggests that several states felt that "students were getting the message that they were not to bring firearms to school and that, as a result, fewer students were expelled for this offense."

Even accepting the veracity of the data, however, it remains unclear what increases or decreases in recovered weapons or expulsions mean in terms of evaluating overall school safety. Reports on zero-tolerance programs have cited both increases and decreases in weapons confiscation and expulsion as evidence of effectiveness.[27] Trends in school expulsion represent an especially ambiguous measure. Although sometimes cited as evidence that a school or a district is cracking down on disruptive students, increased expulsion within a school or school district may well be indicative of a negative trend in school safety. Ultimately, increases or decreases in weapons confiscation or expulsion are meaningful measures of safety only if paired with more direct measures of violence, disruption, or student misbehavior.

Unfortunately, the impact of suspension or expulsion on student behavior or overall school safety has not been directly studied. Yet troubling indirect data suggest that suspension may be ineffective for those students who are most at risk, and most often targeted, for disciplinary consequences. Rates of repeat offending for school suspension are typically quite high, ranging from 35 to 45 percent, suggesting that this segment of the school population is decidedly not getting the message about zero tolerance. Indeed, for some students, suspension is a strong predictor of further suspension, prompting some researchers to conclude that for these students, "suspension functions as a reinforcer . . . rather than as a punisher."[28]

Long-term outcomes associated with suspension are no more reassuring. National studies of school dropout reported that students who had been suspended were three times more likely to drop out of school by their sophomore year than other students; indeed, school disciplinary contact appears to be among the strongest predictors of school dropout.[29]

There may well be unanticipated social costs to this spiral of school exclusion. Research in the field of juvenile delinquency suggests that the strength of the school social bond is an important predictor in explaining delinquency.[30] From a public policy standpoint, one might well question the wisdom of school disciplinary strategies that are expressly intended to break that bond with troublesome students.

Unintended consequences of punishment: Student behavioral and emotional reactions

Student perceptions of the effectiveness of various school disciplinary actions are often significantly at odds with the perceptions of teachers and administrators. While school personnel see school disruption as primarily a student choice and disciplinary consequences as an appropriate reaction to that choice, students, especially at-risk students, tend to view confrontational classroom management or school disciplinary strategies as playing a significant role in escalating student misbehavior, especially if they believe rules or policies are being unfairly applied. In particular, students who are already at risk for disruption may see confrontational discipline as a challenge to escalate their behavior.[31]

Many of these unintended effects may simply reflect the consistent findings of behavioral psychology that the application of punishment is unpredictable and unlikely to lead to the learning of new behavior. A host of serious side effects have been documented in the professional literature on punishment, including escape and counteraggression, habituation to progressively stiffer consequences, and reinforcement of the punishing agent.[32] Unless the application of harsh consequences is carefully monitored and accompanied by positive consequences or alternative goals, it appears to be as likely to lead to escape or counteraggression as to meaningful alternative behavior. The appropriate application of consequences at opportune moments is certainly one tool for teaching students that actions have consequences in a lawful society. Yet it is unclear whether the school punishments central to zero-tolerance policies can be used in a consistent enough manner to yield benefits sufficient to outweigh the well-documented and troubling side effects of punishment procedures.

Does zero tolerance contribute to school safety?

These analyses are in no way intended as a criticism of school administrators faced with complex and serious choices in responding to school violence. The brutal events that overtook suburban and rural schools in the late 1990s have shattered the common belief that school violence is solely an urban problem, confined to bad neighborhoods and dysfunctional families in the inner city.[33] In the space of days and weeks, teachers, administrators, and parents throughout the country were forced to the anxiety-charged realization that violence can happen anywhere. Unprepared for serious violence yet under intense pressure to do something, it is unsurprising that administrators choose remedies, such as zero tolerance and security technology, that they perceive as fast acting. There are few who would disagree with the proposition that schools must take all possible actions to demonstrate their seriousness in deterring violence. Indeed, it is hard to argue with the stated goal of zero tolerance: to send a message that certain behaviors are unacceptable in school.

It is not the goals of zero tolerance, however, but more often the methods of its implementation that create controversy. There are few newspaper editorials condemning schools and school boards for expelling a student who carried a knife or gun to school for the sole purpose of attacking another student. But the classic zero-tolerance strategy of punishing minor or even trivial events severely, or dramatically extending the length of school suspension or expulsion, has led to cries of injustice in communities throughout the nation.

Inevitably, harsher punishments pit proponents of a strong zero-tolerance stance against civil rights advocates. It is not surprising that organizations from both ends of the political spectrum—the American Civil Liberties Union and the conservative Rutherford Institute—have focused on civil rights concerns in defending students caught in the web of zero tolerance. Inevitably, plaintiffs against school districts claim their rights were violated by standard policies that allow for little or no flexibility in implementation. Defenders of the policies point to the larger threat posed by serious violence in the nation's schools, suggesting that civil rights violations may be an unfortunate but necessary compromise to ensure the safety of school environments.

Unfortunately, however, the idea that zero-tolerance policies contribute to improved student behavior or school safety remains unsupported by evidence. Despite more than ten years of implementation in school districts around the country, there is no convincing documentation that zero tolerance has in any way contributed to school safety or improved student behavior. In fact, the implications of available data on disciplinary removal are at best troubling. The contribution of student behavior to suspension or expulsion decisions is swamped by inconsistencies in administration at both the classroom and school levels. For at-risk students, the most consistently documented outcome of suspension and expulsion appears to be further suspension and expulsion, and perhaps school dropout. These relationships are especially troubling in the light of the highly consistent overuse of punishment for African American students, an overrepresentation that cannot be explained away by behavior or the effects of poverty. Together, these data strongly suggest that disciplinary removals do little to ensure school safety and may even make a substantially negative contribution to student behavior or school climate.

Recommendations for equitable and effective discipline

In the wake of deadly violence with firearms in schools, it would be difficult to find advocates for tolerating guns in schools. Yet the overextension of the zero-tolerance paradigm has led to controversy without yielding definitive improvements in school safety. The following recommendations offer alternatives based on best-practice knowledge of what works in school safety and school discipline.

• *Reserve zero-tolerance disciplinary removals for only the most serious and severe of disruptive behaviors, such as weapons offenses, and define those behaviors explicitly.* To avoid community controversy about what constitutes a weapon, any infractions included in a zero-tolerance policy should be well defined, perhaps using a definition drawn from state or federal criminal codes.

• *Replace one-size-fits-all disciplinary strategies with graduated systems of discipline, with consequences geared to the seriousness of the infraction.* In response to community reaction against zero tolerance, many school districts are beginning to move toward reserving severe punishments for serious, safety-threatening offenses. Less serious offenses, such as classroom disruption, attendance-related behaviors, or even minor fights among students, are met with less severe consequences, which might range from in-school suspension to parent contact, reprimands, community service, or counseling.

• *Expand the array of options available to schools for dealing with disruptive or violent behavior.* We must assume that school boards or administrators implementing zero-tolerance policies do not take pleasure in removing children from school. Rather, they simply do not know what else to do. Research on effective preventive alternatives such as bullying prevention, conflict resolution and peer mediation, improved classroom behavior management, and early identification and intervention is critical in order to assist schools in developing sound alternatives to exclusionary discipline. Increased funding that allows school districts to develop a host of violence-prevention strategies is important, as is increased training at the university level in an expanded array of options.

• *Implement preventive measures that can improve school climate and reconnect alienated students.* Solutions to the zero-tolerance dilemma might also seek to shift the focus from swift and certain punishment to improving the sense of school community and belongingness (see Chapter Five, this issue). Indeed, data on a host of preventive measures, ranging from conflict resolution to anger management to bullying prevention, appear to be far more promising than the largely negative findings concerning zero tolerance (see Chapter Four, this issue). Professional opinion has begun to coalesce around a primary prevention model of school violence prevention emphasizing simultaneous intervention at each of three levels.[34] (See Chapters Four through Six of this issue.)

• *Evaluate all school discipline or school violence-prevention strategies to ensure that those strategies are truly having an impact on student behavior and school safety.* Accountability of instruction has become a national priority and must be applied to behavioral and disciplinary procedures as well. The implementation of any procedure addressing student behavior or school violence must be accompanied by an evaluation adequate to determine whether that procedure has made a positive contribution to improving school safety or student behavior. Without such data, there is danger that time and resources will be wasted on strategies that sound appealing but in fact do little to decrease the chances of disruption or violence.

Conclusion: Escaping the cycle of fear

Throughout its brief history, the implementation of and reactions to zero tolerance seem to follow a predictable pattern, one that might be characterized as a cycle of fear. Schools and school districts, responding to fear of increased school violence and disruption, implement harsh measures to reassure the community that action is being taken. Although communities are initially supportive of the apparently decisive new stance, that support soon sours as the civil rights implications of consistently harsh punishments become apparent. Breaking this cycle will require more than a simple reaction to current news events; it will mean assessment of current safety needs, careful planning, implementation of proven effective strategies, and the evaluation of any strategy designed to address violence and disruption.

The dilemma of zero tolerance is profound and serious. We can in no way question the motives or sincerity of those who have drawn a battle line against violence in the schools. Yet however well meaning those policies have been, the pages of national newspapers have been littered with the wreckage of young lives changed, perhaps irrevocably, by policies whose primary aim is to send a message to more serious offenders. Moreover, it has not been substantiated that the antisocial and violent youth who are the intended targets of zero tolerance have in any way received its message. There is yet to be a credible demonstration that zero tolerance has made a significant contribution to school safety or improved student behavior. The tragic violence that has befallen both urban and rural schools makes it incumbent on educators to explore all available means to protect the safety of students and teachers. Yet faced with an almost complete lack of evidence that zero tolerance is among the strategies capable of accomplishing that objective, one can only hope for the development and application of more effective, less intrusive alternatives for preserving the safety of our nation's schools.

Notes

1. Kumar, A. (1999, December 28). Suit fights school alcohol policy. *St. Petersburg Times*, p. 3B; Petrillo, L. (1997, October 29). Eight-year-old may be expelled under zero-tolerance code. *San Diego Union-Tribune*, p. B-1; Borsuk, A. J., & Murphy, M. B. (1999, April 30). Idle or otherwise, threats bring severe discipline: Where area students once faced a principal, now they face the police. *Milwaukee Journal Sentinel*, p. 8; Nancrede, S. F. (1998, August 20).

School to take foul mouths to task: Southport High will institute zero-tolerance policy on profanity. *Indianapolis Star*, p. A1; "Groups critical of no second chances school proposal." (1999, January 27). *Baltimore Sun*, p. 4B; Seymour, L. (1999a, February 24). Getting too tough? Schools are expanding their zero-tolerance policies, disciplining and even kicking out students who misbehave off-campus. *Los Angeles Times*, p. B2.

2. Heaviside, S., Rowand, C., Williams, C., & Farris, E. (1998). *Violence and discipline problems in U.S. public schools: 1996–97*. (NCES 98–030). Washington, DC: U.S. Department of Education, National Center for Education Statistics.

3. Skiba, R. J., & Peterson, R. L. (1999). The dark side of zero tolerance: Can punishment lead to safe schools? *Phi Delta Kappan, 80*, 372–376, 381–382.

4. Kelling, G., & Wilson, J. (1982, March). Broken windows: The police and neighborhood safety. *Atlantic Monthly, 249*(3), 31.

5. Ewing, C. P. (2000, January-February). Sensible zero tolerance protects students. *Harvard Education Letter: Research Online*. Available: www.edletter.org/past/issues/2000-jf/zero-shtml#EWING.

6. In *Violence in America's Public Schools, 1996–97* (Heaviside et al., 1998), schools that reported more day-to-day disciplinary disruptions also reported higher levels of serious crime.

7. Koch, K. (2000). Zero tolerance: Is mandatory punishment in schools unfair? *Congressional Quarterly Researcher, 10*(9), 185–208.

8. The search was conducted using the Lexis-Nexus database entering the term *zero tolerance* under the category "Major Newspapers," for dates ranging from May 1, 1998, to June 1, 2001. See Skiba & Peterson (1999) for an analysis of cases prior to May 1998.

9. In the interest of readability, citations of newspaper articles in this section will be presented in footnotes. For each category, sources are cited in the order of the incidents presented. For weapons incidents, the sources for each incident are: Stepp, D. R. (1999, October 12). Cobb expels student for packing gun. *Atlanta Constitution*, p. 3C; Fitzpatrick, T., Lilly, R., & Houtz, J. (1998, October 6). Schools reverse toy-gun decision: Boy, 11, who was expelled is back at Whitman today. *Seattle Times*, p. B1; Rodriguez, Y. (2000, September 28). Cobb school calls wallet chain a weapon, suspends girl, 11. *Atlanta Constitution*, p. 1A; Second-graders facing charges. (2001, March 22). *Newsday*, p. A33.

10. Drugs and alcohol citations: Abrahms, S. (1998, June 21). Discipline of 9 seniors is evaluated: Headmaster defends "zero tolerance" stance. *Boston Globe*, p. 1; Smith, A. C. (1998, November 14). Court casts doubt on "zero tolerance" policy. *St. Petersburg Times*, p. 1B; Nacelewicz, T. (2001, February 2). Activists file suit after teen expelled: SAD 61 has denied an education to a girl who took pills for a headache, the Maine Civil Liberties Union says. *Portland Press Herald*, p. 1B.

11. Threats: Grenz, C. (2001, March 31). Accused student to return to class. *Topeka Capital-Journal*; Henderson, J. (1999, November 4). Halloween essay lands 13-year-old behind bars: Boy released after news media called. *Houston Chronicle*, p. 1A; Sternberg, N. (2001, April 6). Paranoid times chill fair play. *Chicago Sun-Times*, p. 3.

12. O'Toole, M. E., & the Critical Incident Response Group. (2000). *The school shooter: A threat assessment perspective.* Quantico, VA: Federal Bureau of Investigation. Available: www.fbi.gov/library/school/school2.pdf.

13. At the national level, Heaviside et al. (1998) reported that serious and dangerous behaviors such as weapons possession, physical assault of teacher, and gang-related behavior typically accounted for less than 5 percent of school disciplinary incidents; similar results at the school level were reported in an analysis of middle school disciplinary records by Skiba, R. J., Peterson, R. L., & Williams, T. (1997). Office referrals and suspension: Disciplinary intervention in middle schools. *Education and Treatment of Children, 20*(3), 295–315.

14. In general, courts give broad leeway to school districts regarding discipline. See Zirkel, P. A. (1998). The right stuff. *Phi Delta Kappan, 79*(6), 475–476. But exceptions have been made for due process violation (Lee, C. J. [1999, January 12]. Penn Hills schools lose weapons plea: State court affirms common pleas ruling on expulsion. *Pittsburgh Post Gazette,* p. B-1) or if the policy allows no exceptions (Carney, S. [1998, September 23]. Focus: School district loses on suspension. *Los Angeles Time,* p. B2).

15. Bowditch, C. (1993). Getting rid of troublemakers: High school disciplinary procedures and the production of dropouts. *Social Problems, 40,* 493–507; Rose, T. L. (1988). Current disciplinary practices with handicapped students: Suspensions and expulsions. *Exceptional Children, 55,* 230–239; Skiba et al. (1997); Uchitelle, S., Bartz, D., & Hillman, L. (1989). Strategies for reducing suspensions. *Urban Education, 24,* 163–176.

16. Costenbader, V. K., & Markson, S. (1994). School suspension: A survey of current policies and practices. *NASSP Bulletin, 78,* 103–107; Dupper, D. R., & Bosch, L. A. (1996). Reasons for school suspensions: An examination of data from one school district and recommendations for reducing suspensions. *Journal for a Just and Caring Education, 2,* 140–150; Menacker, J. C., Hurwitz, E., & Weldon, W. (1988). Legislating school discipline: The application of a systemwide discipline code to schools in a large urban district. *Urban Education, 23,* 12–23; Skiba et al. (1997); Cooley, S. (1995). *Suspension/expulsion of regular and special education students in Kansas: A report to the Kansas State Board of Education.* Topeka: Kansas State Board of Education; Kaeser, S. C. (1979). Suspensions in school discipline. *Education and Urban Society, 11,* 465–484; Morgan-D'Atrio, C., Northrup, J., LaFleur, L., & Spera, S. (1996). Toward prescriptive alternatives to suspensions: A preliminary evaluation. *Behavioral Disorders, 21,* 190–200; Imich, A. J. (1994). Exclusions from school: Current trends and issues. *Educational Research, 36*(1), 3–11; Massachusetts Advocacy Center (1986). *The way out: Student exclusion practices in Boston middle schools.* Boston: Author.

17. Wu, S. C., Pink, W. T., Crain, R. L., & Moles, O. (1982). Student suspension: A critical reappraisal. *Urban Review, 14,* 245–303; Tobin, T., Sugai, G., & Colvin, G. (1996). Patterns in middle school discipline records. *Journal of Emotional and Behavioral Disorders, 4*(2), 82–94; Skiba et al. (1997).

18. Eckenrode, J., Laird, M., & Doris, J. (1993). School performance and disciplinary problems among abused and neglected children. *Developmental*

Psychology, 29, 53–62; Morgan-D'Atrio, C., Northrup, J., LaFleur, L., & Spera, S. (1996). Toward prescriptive alternatives to suspensions: A preliminary evaluation. *Behavioral Disorders, 21*, 190–200.

19. Skiba et al. (1997); Bickel, F., & Qualls, R. (1980). The impact of school climate on suspension rates in the Jefferson County Public Schools. *Urban Review, 12*, 79–86; Davis, J. E., & Jordan, W. J. (1994). The effects of school context, structure, and experiences on African American males in middle and high schools. *Journal of Negro Education, 63*, 570–587; Hellman, D. A., & Beaton, S. (1986). The pattern of violence in urban public schools: The influence of school and community. *Journal of Research in Crime and Delinquency, 23*, 102–127; Wu et al. (1982).

20. Brantlinger, E. (1991). Social class distinctions in adolescents' reports of problems and punishment in school. *Behavioral Disorders, 17*, 36–46; Skiba et al. (1997); Wu et al. (1982).

21. Costenbader & Markson (1994). Glackman, T., Martin, R., Hyman, I., McDowell, E., Berv, V., & Spino, P. (1978). Corporal punishment, school suspension, and the civil rights of students: An analysis of Office for Civil Rights school surveys. *Inequality in Education, 23*, 61–65; Kaeser, S. C. (1979). Suspensions in school discipline. *Education and Urban Society, 11*, 465–484; Lietz, J. J., & Gregory, M. K. (1978). Pupil race and sex determinants of office and exceptional education referrals. *Educational Research Quarterly, 3*(2), 61–66; McCarthy, J. D., & Hoge, D. R. (1987). The social construction of school punishment: Racial disadvantage out of universalistic process. *Social Forces, 65*, 1101–1120; McFadden, A. C., Marsh, G. E., Price, B. J., & Hwang, Y. (1992). A study of race and gender bias in the punishment of handicapped school children. *Urban Review, 24*, 239–251; Skiba et al. (1997); Taylor, M. C., & Foster, G. A. (1986). Bad boys and school suspensions: Public policy implications for black males. *Sociological Inquiry, 56*, 498–506; Thornton, C. H., & Trent, W. (1988). School desegregation and suspension in East Baton Rouge Parish: A preliminary report. *Journal of Negro Education, 57*, 482–501; Wu et al. (1982); Shaw, S. R., & Braden, J. P. (1990). Race and gender bias in the administration of corporal punishment. *School Psychology Review, 19*, 378–383.

22. McFadden et al. (1992); Tailor, H., & Detch, E. R. (1998). *Getting tough on kids: A look at zero tolerance.* Nashville: Tennessee Office of Education Accountability, Comptroller of the Treasury; Gordon, R., Piana, L. D., & Keleher, T. (2000). *Facing the consequences: An examination of racial discrimination in U.S. public schools.* Oakland, CA: Applied Research Center.

23. National Association of Secondary School Principals (2000, February). *Statement on civil rights implications of zero tolerance programs.* Testimony presented to the U.S. Commission on Civil Rights, Washington, DC; Wu et al. (1982); Skiba et al. (2000)

24. McCarthy & Hoge (1987); Wu et al. (1982); McFadden et al. (1992); Shaw & Braden (1990).

25. Skiba, R. J., Michael, R. S., Nardo, A. C., & Peterson, R. L. (in press). The color of discipline: Sources of racial and gender disproportionality in school punishment. *Urban Review.*

26. Sinclair, B. (1999). *Report on state implementation of the Gun-Free Schools Act: School Year 1997–98*. Rockville, MD: Westat.

27. Crosby, J. (1994, December 18). "Zero tolerance" makes its mark: Expulsions in Orange County schools have tripled since 1990. *Orange County Register*, p. A1; Barzewski, L. (1997, November 18). Weapons at school on decline: New figures show tough policy works. *Fort Lauderdale Sun-Sentinel*, p. 1A; Ginsberg, C. G., & Loffredo, L. (1993). Violence-related attitudes and behaviors of high school students—New York City, 1992. *Morbidity and Mortality Weekly Report, 42*, 773–777.

28. Bowditch (1993); Costenbader & Markson (1994); Tobin et al. (1996). p. 91.

29. Ekstrom, R. B., Goertz, M. E., Pollack, J. M., & Rock, D. A. (1986). Who drops out of high school and why? Findings from a national study. *Teachers College Record, 87*, 357–73; Wehlage, G. G., & Rutter, R. A. (1986). Dropping out: How much do schools contribute to the problem? *Teachers College Record, 87*, 374–393.

30. Jenkins, P. H. (1997). School delinquency and the school social bond. *Journal of Research in Crime and Delinquency, 34*, 337–367.

31. Gottfredson, D. G. (1989). Developing effective organizations to reduce school disorder. In O. C. Moles (Ed.), *Strategies to reduce student misbehavior*. Washington, D.C.: Office of Educational Research and Improvement. (ERIC Document Reproduction Service No. ED 311 608); Shores, R. E, Gunter, P. L., & Jack, S. L. (1993). Classroom management strategies: Are they setting events for coercion? *Behavioral Disorders, 18*, 92–102.

32. Skinner, B. F. (1953). *Science and human behavior*. New York: Free Press; Council for Exceptional Children. (1991). *Reducing undesirable behaviors* (CEC Mini-Library: Working with Behavioral Disorders). Reston, VA: Council for Exceptional Children; Axelrod, S., & Apsche, J. (1983). *The effects of punishment on human behavior*. New York: Academic Press; MacMillan, D. L., Forness, S. R., & Trumball, B. M. (1973). The role of punishment in the classroom. *Exceptional Children, 40*, 85–96; Wood, F. H., & Braaten, S. (1983). Developing guidelines for the use of punishing interventions in the schools. *Exceptional Education Quarterly, 3*(4), 68–75.

33. Prothrow-Stith, D., & Weissman, M. (1991). *Deadly consequences: How violence is destroying our teenage population and a plan to begin solving the problem*. New York: HarperCollins.

34. American Psychological Association. (1993). *Violence and youth: Psychology's response* (Vol. 1). Washington, DC: Author; Dwyer, K., Osher, D., & Warger, C. (1998). *Early warning, timely response: A guide to safe schools*. Washington, DC: U.S. Department of Education; Walker, H. M., Horner, R. H., Sugai, G., Bullis, M., Sprague, J. R., Bricker, D., & Kaufman, M. J. (1996). Integrated approaches to preventing antisocial behavior patterns among school-age children and youth. *Journal of Emotional and Behavioral Disorders, 4*(4), 194–209.

RUSSELL J. SKIBA *is associate professor of counseling and educational psychology at Indiana University and director of the Safe and Responsive Schools Project.*

KIMBERLY KNESTING *is assistant professor of psychology at the University of Wisconsin-Eau Claire.*

A better understanding of expulsion as an act, a process, and an educational intervention leads to an entirely different understanding of student behavior and disciplinary consequences.

2

School expulsion as a process and an event: Before and after effects on children at risk for school discipline

Gale M. Morrison, Suzanne Anthony, Meri H. Storino, Joanna J. Cheng, Michael J. Furlong, Richard L. Morrison

PUBLIC EDUCATION is faced with the ever-increasing challenge of educating all children to meet high standards in the contexts of limited school resources and communities of families and children with complex needs and problems. Teachers are confronted with students who represent a significant range of needs and abilities. Noncompliance and misbehavior add yet another level of complexity to teaching situations, and the developmental safety of students may be threatened in situations where misbehavior disrupts the classroom process. School officials must also maintain safe and orderly campuses; physical safety of students is key to a productive learning environment. Yet a certain number of students will always present ongoing challenges to orderly learning environments. How

NEW DIRECTIONS FOR YOUTH DEVELOPMENT, NO. 92, WINTER 2001 © WILEY PERIODICALS, INC.

do school systems deal with this type of diversity? The easy answer, all too often used, is to exclude the offenders.

The 1960s brought public law and legislation to prevent public schools from excluding diversity due to disability. Interestingly, social and behavioral maladjustment, without a parallel learning or emotional disability, is not covered by existing federal disability definitions. Debate continues about whether schools are obligated to educate students who egregiously and continually violate school rules. Walker and his colleagues conceptualize this social policy conflict as a result of the competing worldviews representing what they refer to as a constrained view (humans are imperfect; they misbehave, are responsible for that misbehavior, and should pay the consequences) and an unconstrained view (humans are perfectible; they misbehave due to special causes, ignorance, or social inequities; special circumstances require individualized application of consequences).[1]

Exclusion remains the intervention of choice, under the constrained worldview for students who violate school rules and are not officially identified as disabled. The assumption remains that somehow these students should lose their right to a public education if they cannot abide by the behavioral parameters set by schools. In contrast, under the unconstrained view, students with disabilities are afforded the protection of continued education under the assumption that severe rule violations are related to their disability; their educational needs and rights remain in the face of expellable offenses. In the one case, the obligation to educate a student ends; in the other case, it does not. In the one case, expulsion is an event that ends the educational right; in the other, the educational process continues, albeit with changes to accommodate the needs and behaviors of the student.

In this chapter, we examine school expulsion, the ultimate punishment for rules violations, as both a process and an event. The characteristics of students who are involved in expulsion processes are discussed, and we consider the effectiveness (if not the wisdom) of expulsion, the event, as an educational intervention. We frame our consideration of school expulsion, the event, with the processes and contexts that lead to and result from the act of excluding students from a school when they have committed an expellable offense.

Definitions

School expulsion is the ultimate weapon of zero tolerance. A zero-tolerance policy is defined as a school or district policy that mandates predetermined consequences or punishment for specific offenses, regardless of the circumstances or disciplinary history of the student involved. States, paralleling the federal Gun-Free Schools Act (GFSA) of 1994, generally create guidelines for districts to implement zero-tolerance policies; those districts may exceed but not ignore such guidelines. Nationally, nine of ten schools reported zero-tolerance policies for firearms (94 percent) and weapons other than firearms (91 percent), for alcohol (87 percent), and for drugs (88 percent). Most schools had zero-tolerance policies for violence (79 percent) and tobacco possession (79 percent).[2]

Expellable offenses

We use California's policy as an example of a state mandate for zero tolerance. The California Legislature enacted zero-tolerance laws that called for a mandatory expulsion recommendation for students who committed any of the following acts, unless the punishment was considered inappropriate for the circumstance of the act: (1) causing serious physical injury to another person, except in self-defense; (2) possession of any knife, explosive, or other dangerous object of no reasonable use to the pupil; (3) unlawful possession of a controlled substance, except for the first offense of less than one ounce of marijuana; (4) robbery or extortion; or (5) assault or battery. Although these offenses require a recommendation for expulsion, for numerous others, suspension or expulsion may be used; the latest addition to this list is "terroristic threats against school officials, school property, or both."[3]

Results of the expulsion action

Information on the disciplinary actions taken by school districts for specific offenses is available in national databases. In the case of firearm possession, 94 percent of schools reported they followed a zero-tolerance policy toward firearms, but only 31 percent reported they actually expelled students for this offense. Of the remaining districts, when a firearm violation occurred, 49 percent used a suspension of five or more days, and 20 percent transferred students to other programs or schools.[4] This pattern indicates the likelihood that districts were using some discretion in the final decision about consequences for students, a trend also seen in data from the GFSA report.[5]

In fact, there are a number of possible outcomes of an initial recommendation to expel; several of these options result in no expulsion, thereby removing the incident from the realm of district reporting and statistics. The district may decide to suspend the expulsion action; this constitutes a suspended order. Under a suspended order, the expulsion process is completed, but the enforcement of the expulsion is suspended. A suspended order may occur if it is determined that keeping the student within the district's programs is appropriate. Often this means a transfer to another school or specialized program for a specified and agreed-on period of time. Alternatively, the student may return to the host campus, especially when he or she is already at an alternative setting. The district may also drop the expulsion action completely. This decision is often based on the failure of school administrators to follow procedures of due process correctly, thereby weakening the district's case for expulsion and exposing the district to possible legal action and appeals if the expulsion recommendation is acted on. Cases may also be undermined by weak evidence or unsubstantiated allegations. The expulsion case may involve a student with a documented disability, in which case further investigation is needed and may result in the expulsion action being dropped (if the incident is related to the disability or appropriate education was not being provided). Finally, the expulsion action may be completed and the student transferred to an alternative school setting outside the district.

The expulsion process therefore may lead to a variety of outcomes—for example, the student enrolls in an out-of-district program, a court or community school, home teaching, a private school, or no school setting whatsoever, in effect dropping out. In California, the district has an obligation to refer a student to an appropriate program, although this is not the case for all states. Thus, a consideration of the school expulsion as an event must recognize the variety of outcomes for individual students. National and state statistics do not reflect this variation and often are not accompanied by clear methodological explanations about which cases have been included in reported numbers.

Expulsion rates

Despite the social and personal significance of expulsion from school, research focused on this phenomenon is surprisingly sparse. What is available shows a dramatic increase in the use of exclusions and expulsions as a final disciplinary measure.[6] Reporting practices typically include number of suspensions in the same phrase as expulsions; therefore, information about expulsions alone is more limited than about combined disciplinary measures. However, some of the following figures are available for expulsions only. For example, the Chicago schools reported a dramatic increase in expulsions; from 1992 to 1999 (academic years), the number of expulsions cases increased from 14 to 737.[7] Massachusetts saw a 35 percent increase in the number of expulsions from 1993 to 1997.[8] Interestingly, students were expelled more often for nonviolent offenses (only

9 percent had a gun; 25 percent had a weapon other than a gun or knife). And a suburban district in California experienced a dramatic rise in school expulsion recommendations, from just 2 in 1991–92 to 83 in 1994–95.[9]

Massachusetts data also reflect differences in urban versus suburban and small school districts in expulsion rates, with suburban and smaller school districts outstripping their urban counterparts. After the passage of GFSA (which requires states to have legislation mandating the expulsion of youths who bring guns to school), the number of students expelled dropped from 5,724 students in 1996–97 to 3,930 during the next year, according to Brooks, Schiraldi, and Ziedenberg, who proffer two possible explanations for the decrease: (1) a drop in delinquency or (2) the effectiveness of zero tolerance as a deterrent.[10] The drop may also be due to the increased ability of school administrators to find flexibility within an essentially inflexible policy.

Characteristics of students who are expelled

Through the examination of the characteristics of students who are expelled, we may come to understand the reasons for their misbehavior and the paths that bring them, over time, to commit serious school rule violations. There are sparse data available on the characteristics of students who get expelled; much more information exists about students who are suspended. The confound in actually separating these two types of school discipline measures is that before a student is expelled, the interim arrangement is suspension. Therefore, suspension data likely include students who (1) eventually get expelled or (2) who, although recommended for expulsion, are not actually expelled, and (3) students who are suspended for lesser offenses.

Morrison and D'Incau examined one district's expulsion cases over a two-year period.[11] They found that the expelled students had different educational and behavioral profiles; only a small percentage had significant disciplinary histories. Other groups consisted of students who got caught in one-time offenses that did not fit their overall school behavior pattern, were showing signs of disconnection from school in terms of attendance and performance but were not disruptive, or were served at some point by special education and were experiencing learning and behavioral problems. Thus, students who were unlikely to pose a serious threat or danger to the school environment committed the majority of the disciplinary offenses. These students had taken different pathways to the expulsion event and had strikingly different etiologies to explain their behavior: attendance problems, school disconnection, involvement in drugs, or a chronic history of emotional difficulties. Notably, students recommended for expulsion were performing well below average in terms of grades and achievement scores. Thus, the one common red flag was poor school performance.

Minority and special needs populations

Data about suspensions and expulsions are consistent in the characterization of the overrepresentation of minority students and students with special needs (see Chapter Three, this issue). Here we note some trends for special needs students. Students with special education needs are caught often "in the web of zero tolerance."[12] Case histories and demographic descriptions of excluded students have revealed a heterogeneous group, very few of whom presented real or serious dangers to students or staff.[13] In Massachusetts in 1996–97, 25 percent of the children expelled were previously enrolled in special education programs, even though they represented 15 percent of the state's school enrollment.[14] The U.S. General Accounting Office (GAO) surveyed 272 public and high school administrators about incidents of serious misconduct in their schools during the 1999–2000 academic year and the representation of regular and special education students in these incidents.[15] Principals reported an average of fourteen incidents during the school year, four involving special education students. Controlling for the differential representation of regular and special education students in schools, the ratio of serious misconduct by students is 15 per 1,000 for regular education students and 50 per 1,000 for special education students. These incidents of misconduct include both suspensions and expulsions. Information on expulsions given in the GAO report was limited to a statement that about one in six of the cases of serious misconduct resulted in expulsions, the rate for regular and special education students being approximately equal. This rate was characterized as relatively low. While a majority of special education students received educational services after the expulsion, only about 50 percent of the regular education students received services.

The one group that was overrepresented in the Morrison and D'Incau study was students with disabilities.[16] Twenty-five percent of the sample was previously, currently, or would soon be identified as having a disability that qualified them for special education; this rate is about twice what would be expected in the population at large. The majority of special education students in this sample were in the "troubled" group, their records identifying chronic emotional and familial problems evident from the early elementary years.

Expulsion: Process leading to the event

In an intensive examination of school expulsion cases involving students with disabilities, Morrison and D'Incau revealed a picture of a heterogeneous group with varied developmental trajectories that preceded the expulsion offense; very few in this group presented real or serious dangers to students or staff.[17] However, all cases showed evidence of documented emotional, familial, or behavioral risk indicators that paralleled their special education histories. Particularly salient risks for students included a history of attention deficit hyperactivity disorder or conduct problems, chronic or crisis-related family problems, and a history of inconsistent special education placements and interventions. In the cases where special education was a consistent presence in the student's life, the placement and the teacher served as a protective factor against disciplinary action.

One critical point of the Morrison and D'Incau study was that student developmental and behavioral trajectories were inextricably tied together. A student's characteristics and ensuing behaviors interact transactionally with the ongoing attempts by school officials to provide the most appropriate education possible. Lack of consistent and appropriate programming, education, and treatment exacerbates the student's developmental problems. School expulsion can act as either an exit or an entrance to appropriate education. Three common scenarios were found. One was characterized by cases of students who were decertified, that is, found ineligible for special education services; these students often had associated conduct problems. The decertification made it easier for school officials to expel without the constraints of the process required in the Individuals with Disabilities Education Act (IDEA) Amendments of 1997.[18] In these instances, the student exited both special and regular education for some type of alternative educational setting. A report from the California Youth Authority (CYA) revealed a similar trend; that is, it was standard practice to decertify special education eligibility for remanded youth.[19] It took a court ruling in 1994 to direct the CYA to provide special education resources in its schools. In the second scenario, the manifestation, determination, and assessment of appropriate education found no relationship between the disability and the offense, and a determination was made that the student was receiving appropriate special education services. Again, the student exited both special and regular education systems. When the offense was related to the disability and the placement was appropriate, special education services were continued in the same school environment. In the final scenario, although the student had been experiencing school adjustment problems for years, no special education had been provided. After the incident leading to expulsion, the student was assessed and determined eligible for services under the "emotional disturbance" eligibility category and then was transferred to a school or class that offered special education services and support.

Expulsion is a process, not merely an event. Evidence suggests that when a student commits an expellable offense at school, it is often not a surprise in the context of his or her developmental history. Although not all students follow the same developmental or disciplinary history in their path to breaking school rules, many have case histories that suggest difficulties with school and family adjustment. By viewing expulsion as merely an event, and thus not considering what led the student to behave in this fashion, we limit our ability to match appropriate consequences and future effective interventions.

Factors protecting against expulsion

The factors associated with how students arrive at the expulsion event typically are framed as risk factors—that is, they have risks in areas of ethnic minority status, disability, school maladjustment, lack of parent advocacy, and alienation from school activities and people.[20] Another reason to consider expulsion as a process is that for students recommended for school expulsion, the final consequence may not be expulsion. Protective factors in a student's life could increase the possibility that alternatives to expulsion would be used as consequences for the student's offense.[21] For example, a student whose parent was a lawyer was likely to avoid the expulsion decision, especially when all due process procedures may not have been strictly implemented. Another influence that decreased the possibility of expulsion was the presence of a school or community advocate. These individuals generally vouched for the overall character of the student and advocated for continuity for him or her in current educational and therapeutic interventions. A student with multiple positive factors in his or her school record (such as extramural activities, leadership roles, or good grades) was less likely to receive the full expulsion consequence. Finally, special education services and support served as a deterrent to school expulsion (beyond the initial recommendation), especially given the protections provided to special education students under IDEA.

School-level influences on pathways to expulsion

The consideration of risk and protective factors in the process of school expulsion necessitates an examination of school-level influences. A school's environment may present students with challenges or assistance in the development and maintenance of appropriate school behavior. "Get-tough" school expulsion policies are perhaps the inappropriate extension of the practice of clear and public high expectations for student learning and behavior, a critical correlate of effective schools. Other effective school correlates are clear and focused school mission, instructional leadership, a safe and orderly school environment, opportunities for learning and student academic engagement, frequent monitoring and feedback in regard to student performance, and positive home-school relations.[22] In contrast to effective schools, schools with a high incidence of school violence and disruption are associated with the following characteristics: rules are unclear or perceived as unfairly or inconsistently enforced, students do not believe in the rules, teachers and administrators do not know what the rules are or disagree on the proper responses to student misconduct, cooperation between teachers and the school administration is poor or the administration is inactive, teachers tend to have punitive attitudes, and misconduct is ignored.[23]

The disciplinary environment of a school is another possible influence on the number of offenses committed by students on a campus. Morrison, Morrison, and Minjarez suggest that the principal's philosophy about and skill in handling behavioral transgressions directly influences the number of suspensions at the school level.[24] Administrators with a broader view of the influences on child behavior were able to create additional educational and personal-social interventions to support future positive behavior rather than depend on punitive interventions. Thus, child characteristics interact with school discipline philosophy to create differential outcomes for students with behavioral challenges. The Civil Rights Project report on zero tolerance noted that "a meaningful approach to school discipline is one that treats students and their families with respect throughout the process, seeks to learn from students and to nurture their learning and growth as human beings, and that find ways to bring students more deeply into the school community."[25] Thus, school characteristics need to be considered in the understanding of how a student comes to a school expulsion event.

The aftermath: Consequences of the expulsion process

In the light of the large and obviously growing number of students expelled from school, it is increasingly important to investigate the consequences of this action. Unfortunately, little is known about what happens to students after they are expelled. Many psychologists and educators are concerned, however, about the negative impact that exclusionary procedures such as expulsion are likely to have on youth.

Disciplinary processes like expulsion that punish children rather than instruct or assist them appear in direct conflict with many of the developmental needs of school-age students, specifically the need to develop strong and trusting relationships with adults and the need to form positive attitudes about fairness and justice. The following example illustrates how the expulsion process can interrupt the fulfillment of these two needs. In a Kansas high school, a student was searched due to suspicion of marijuana use. School officials, whom he trusted, told him that if he told the truth about his marijuana use, "things would go easy on him." Unfortunately, this was not the case. The student told the truth but still received the maximum punishment: a 186-day expulsion. His mother stated, "Not once did anyone ask if he [my son] was OK or did they ask if he needed help and suggest counseling. None of this was offered. Only punishment, no help." This student realized that he made a mistake, but he and his family were left feeling misled, "treated less than human," and as if "no one cared."[26]

Expelling a child from school may act to alienate him or her further from the learning environment and those in it and may even intensify those troubling behaviors targeted for elimination. Mayer found that coercive and punitive disciplinary measures implemented by the school system actually contribute to antisocial behavior in youth.[27] In fact, students with behavior problems who are expelled are at greater risk of committing delinquent acts because they are not in school, do not receive needed treatment, are often left unsupervised, and have more opportunities to socialize with deviant peers, carry a weapon, engage in sexual intercourse, and use tobacco, alcohol, and illicit substances.[28] Unfortunately, many youth who are excluded from schools become involved with the juvenile justice system. Often, the only other young people available for them to form social bonds with are other troubled peers living in similarly difficult, unsupportive circumstances.[29]

In addition to these negative outcomes, exclusionary procedures have been linked to academic failure. Students who are suspended or expelled have higher school dropout rates.[30] In fact, being suspended or expelled was rated among the top three school-related reasons for dropping out.[31] Students who are suspended or expelled from school are often already struggling with the day-to-day academic and social demands placed on them in the educational setting. Removing them from academic and social instruction on a long-term basis can create a downward spiral, which may ultimately lead to their dropping out of school entirely.

The expulsion process can exacerbate existing difficulties and also create new challenges resulting in school failure. High school students who are expelled lose academic credits toward graduation and as a result are often retained, a factor that has been linked to school failure. Many students who are expelled from school may lose access to needed transportation, thus making it impossible to attend alternative education programs. In Mississippi, five students were expelled for throwing peanuts at each other and accidentally hitting the bus driver with one.[32] All five students lost their right to ride the district's school buses; due to their economic and geographical circumstances, they were unable to secure a ride to their alternative education placement. Consequently, all five students dropped out of school. The consequences of school expulsion for students in high school are thus potentially extreme and far-reaching in the scheme of their schooling.

Students with disabilities appear to be at even greater risk for the devastating effects of these exclusionary procedures. Special education students are disproportionately more likely to drop out of school as a result of suspension and expulsion than students who are not receiving special education services. Studies have shown that 27 percent of all special education students who drop out were previously absent from school for thirty days or more.[33] When students with disabilities are expelled, their education is disrupted, they fall further behind academically, and they consequently become even more disconnected and frustrated with the educational system and drop out. Students with disabilities are also at risk for losing needed special education services if they are expelled after determining that their offense is not related to their disability and that they had been receiving appropriate education and support.

Although there is little research documenting the consequences of the expulsion process, available information seems to indicate that such exclusionary procedures have a detrimental effect on all students. After expulsion, students without disabilities often do not receive the educational or social services that they so desperately need. Many states have begun to make alternative education programs available to students who are expelled.

Alternative education options

Educational options for students who are expelled from school are limited. Alternative education programs often provide services to students who have been expelled, but not all students who are expelled are afforded the right to attend these programs. There are no federal laws mandating that all states provide alternative education placement for students who are expelled. Currently, the decision as to whether these alternative programs are discretionary or mandatory in nature varies state by state. Unfortunately, there is some evidence that expelled students may not receive alternative education. During 1997–98 in Massachusetts, 37 percent of students who were expelled did not receive alternative education, mainly due to the school district's decision.[34]

A common educational option in California for students who have been expelled from local schools is a county-level community school. However, most do not accept youth from elementary schools and often do not accept students from middle or junior high schools. If programs are available for preadolescent students, issues of transporting these younger students to county schools facilities become a barrier to their actual attendance in that these facilities are often miles from their home school and neighborhood. As zero-tolerance policies are implemented with younger students (recently in New Jersey, two elementary students were excluded after playing with paper guns), this dearth of options for alternative settings becomes critical. This mismatch of policy and educational options demonstrates the operation of a constrained worldview.

Alternative education began as a social movement in the 1960s to empower poor and minority students and is often defined as "an educational program that embraces subject matter and/or teaching methodology that is not generally offered to students of the same age or grade level in traditional school settings, which offers a range of educational options and includes the students as an integral part of the planning team." Alternative programs usually incorporate a vocational component, basic skill instruction, an emphasis on high school completion, opportunities for teacher mentoring through daily interaction, and parent education programs. According to a recent survey, alternative education programs usually serve students who are pregnant, homeless, migrant, delinquent, disruptive, in need of remedial education, or have been expelled, suspended, or released from correctional facilities.

Perhaps due to the wide variety of students served, as well as the differing legislation across states regarding implementation of programs, very little is known about how well alternative education placements serve students, particularly those who have been expelled.[35] In a review of over fifty evaluations of alternative schools in the United States, investigators found little empirical evidence that alternative schools decrease delinquent behavior. They did find, however, that students' attitudes toward school significantly improved, with students reporting that they preferred alternative to traditional schools. Specific programs have made claims that their alternative education programs have had some success in providing general equivalency diploma completion, remedial assistance, and vocational training; developing communication, coping, and self-control skills; and keeping students in school.[36] For example, one alternative education program in New York reported success using individualized programming for students and on-site supervision and mentoring. Over the course of two years, 65 percent of students maintained 100 percent attendance, completed assigned internships, and earned high school diplomas.[37]

Legal and policy implications for expulsion as an event

The legal and due process procedures that surround school expulsion are derived from case law and state legislation.[38] Since GFSA, state laws regarding school expulsion have increased exponentially. For example, the Student Support Services Division of the Los Angeles County Schools publishes an annual update on expulsion laws that now is more than eighty single-spaced pages.[39] These laws cover such issues as what qualifies as an expulsion offense, due process hearing requirements, provision of educational alternatives, and appeal procedures.

The increase in the use of school expulsions has led to a number of legal complications for administering school districts. These legal issues center around due process, constitutional issues such as the First Amendment (free speech) and Fourteenth Amendment (education as a property right), fair and consistent enforcement of the policy, and interaction with the mandates of IDEA (see Chapter Three, this issue, for a discussion of legal issues). One expert in California reported that the main appeals issue facing a large county schools office is that site-based school officials do not know how to build "evidence-based cases" and conduct hearings about expulsion matters (P. Kauble, personal communication, Mar. 9, 2001). Not surprisingly, these officials are not lawyers, and yet they are being asked to conduct complex legal procedures. These matters become even more complicated legal issues for school officials when the expulsion recommendation involves a student with special needs protected under the provisions of IDEA.

Expulsion as social control or consequence for individual behavior

Part of the problem surrounding the use of zero-tolerance expulsions is that what starts as a public statement to the community of students and parents (we will not tolerate x, y, or z) ends up in use for individual cases that invariably present a multitude of extenuating circumstances and causes. Hence, a group mandate becomes an individual's quagmire. In its strictest interpretation, the California Education Code, for example, does not encourage the unthinking application of policy to individuals; that is, a student can be suspended or expelled only after two criteria are met: (1) the student presents a continuing danger to others at the school or threatens to disrupt the instructional process, and (2) other means of correction fail to bring about proper conduct. These criteria are designed to ensure that each case is treated individually. Yet the implementation of zero tolerance still leaves room for seemingly arbitrary and capricious decisions by school officials under the guise of zero-tolerance policies (for example, the flurry of expulsions for students wearing trench coats and other suspicious apparel after the Columbine shootings). The American Bar Association recently passed a resolution in opposition to schools' zero-tolerance disciplinary policies that fail to take into account the circumstances or nature of an offense or an accused student's history.[40] They supported three principles concerning schools discipline: (1) schools should have strong policies against gun possession and be safe places for students to learn and develop; (2) in cases involving alleged students' misbehavior, school officials should exercise sound discretion that is consistent with principles of due process and considers the individual student and the particular circumstances of misconduct; and (3) alternatives to expulsion or referral for prosecution should be developed that will improve student behavior and school climate without making schools dangerous.

The aftermath of the March 2001 shooting in Santee, California, is an example of how highly publicized school violence affects the implementation of zero-tolerance policies. Several weeks before the shooting, the *Los Angeles Times* reported that some school districts "quietly" were "easing rules on discipline."[41] Reasons for these changes were the need to replace harsh and restrictive policies with procedures that allow administrators greater discretion and judgment in dealings with students who break zero-tolerance rules and prevent some of the unintended individual consequences of restrictive expulsion policies such as negative and unerasable marks on a student's record. Several weeks after the Santee incident, the *Los Angeles Times* reported that an Orange County school board was scheduled to give approval to a zero-tolerance approach to bullying that was to cover verbal and physical abuse.[42] Citing the parallel that bullying was associated with some of the high-profile shootings in the country, one board member was quoted, "We felt this was something that was long overdue, and we've got to break the code of silence." This is another example of an attempt to give a social message through zero-tolerance applications to individual offenses. Interestingly, on the same newspaper page was an article about two thousand students skipping classes after e-mails that warned that a student planned to shoot up their campus.

Obviously, the threats and bullying are distressing and need attention and consequence, but how do we balance the need for policies that are intended for social control (communication of expectations) with the need to tailor reasonable consequences for the misbehavior of individuals? This balance is extremely difficult to achieve in the context of the drama created by school shootings and reinforced by extensive media coverage. Administrators and school board members are caught up in the cycle of public opinion and outcry for safety when bad events occur. Under these conditions, school leaders are more likely to react quickly by resorting to prespecified, reactive strategies in an attempt to stabilize their school community and deal with public relations fallout. However, when confronted with the individual case circumstances of students who have broken school rules, it is easier to react with fairness and sensitivity. Thus, the public versus the individual perspectives implies different purposes and outcomes.

Expulsion serves multiple purposes for events that have multiple causes. Table 2.1 outlines the purposes of expulsion under the constrained and the unconstrained worldviews. These purposes vary, depending on who the target of the policy is intended to be. It is difficult to imagine that the expulsion process as now conceived could meet all needs in all circumstances. Thus, it is important to clarify the purposes, the target, and the desired outcome of processes that we put in place in public schools. To begin to sort out the confusions of the zero-tolerance controversy, it will probably be necessary to distinguish between providing consequences for individual actions and suggesting norms for public behavior.

Table 2.1. Potential audiences and desired outcomes for school expulsion policies

| | | Targets of Impact of Explosion | |
Perspective	Youth	School	Community
Constrained (punishment without consideration of special circumstances)	Punishment of youth, experience of consequences	Deterrence and maintenance of school safety	Maintenance of social control and protection of positive public relations
Unconstrained (punish with consideration of special circumstances)	Rehabilitation and link to appropriate services	Maintain enhanced climate for learning	Proactive problem prevention and building confidence in schools

Recommendations

Following are recommendations for developing a better understanding of expulsion as an act, a process, and an educational intervention.

- *Replace zero-tolerance policies with a reasoned and appropriate approach to school discipline.* Educators need to articulate best practices in school discipline and to what purposes these practices are put. This means they need to consider and decide on which side of the constrained and unconstrained view of misbehavior that they fall—that is, standing by a commitment to educating all youth according to their identified needs (unconstrained) or at some point excluding students because their needs and behavior are outside some predetermined boundary (constrained). This does not imply that all youth can or should be educated in a general school setting, but it does imply that no youth will be cut loose without carefully evaluating educational options with an eye toward helping them to reconstruct their relationships with adults.[43]

The development of a reasoned and appropriate approach to school discipline will take time and money. The lack of time and money may be the source of everything that is bad about school expulsion. School personnel need to reflect on and choose strategies for their school discipline system. Although there are good examples available of the general parameters of a proactive discipline approach, schools must match strategies to their school community. This process takes time—time away from the instructional and academic work of the school. Finding this time amid demands for increasingly stringent academic standards and school accountability is challenging, especially in a context of roller-coaster ebb and flow of public opinion and reaction to high-profile incidents of school violence.

The American Bar Association recommendations contain three critical ingredients for a sound approach to school discipline. They emphasize the need for a safe and orderly campus, the importance of considering cases on an individual basis, and the advisability of having multiple educational options. In some ways, they mirror the emphasis in this chapter of considering the process leading up to the misbehavior, the rule-breaking event, and the aftermath. The recommendations that follow touch on each of these areas.

• *Support and implement comprehensive prevention programs to enhance the protective nature of schools.* The view of expulsion as a process recognizes that prevention programs should be available and comprehensive to address student needs before their behavior flags a crisis. The federal document *Safeguarding Our Children* outlines a three-level approach to preventing school violence that suggests differential approaches and program intensity depending on the specific needs and characteristics of the student subgroup.[44] For example, most students will be able to function in school within a specified set of school rules and expectations. A smaller but significant subset of students will need more explicit guidance and benefit from proactive approaches to school discipline, such as clear expectations for behavior and the opportunity to learn and practice conflict resolution skills. A small group of students will require structured behavioral interventions such as the behavior intervention plans suggested under IDEA. The implementation of an integrated, comprehensive school discipline plan requires concerted planning and systematic training of personnel at the school. Schoolwide discipline strategies should become an integral part of preservice and in-service training of teachers, administrators, school psychologists, and school counselors. Classified personnel can also play a supportive role in school discipline and should be included in on-site training efforts.

In the case of students with disabilities and those who are experiencing learning, social, or emotional problems but are not eligible for services under IDEA, every effort should be made to meet their special needs through coordinated and consistent service delivery. Ignoring problems or exposing students to chaotic and uncoordinated interventions does not serve these students in the long run. Students with disabilities may receive psychological services from a school psychologist, but these professionals are typically understaffed and have assessment loads that preclude their intervening in meaningful ways with students who may need their services. Collaboration between mental health professionals within the school and the community is necessary to meet the needs of students who are struggling with school adjustment.

• *Develop alternative discipline strategies to replace school expulsion, and offer educational options when expulsion may be necessary.* Effective alternatives to school exclusion should be examined. In-school suspension is becoming increasingly popular. Although this option keeps students in school (and schools are able to claim attendance funding for these students), this practice should be examined for effectiveness. Additional options to school exclusion should be developed and evaluated for effectiveness.

Not all students can survive in traditional educational settings. The availability of appropriate educational options for these students, who represent a minority of the overall student population, may save the overall student population from the disruptive forces that these few students may generate. These students should be afforded the opportunity to thrive in settings that address their special needs. Alternative educational settings have increased without the benefit of well-researched best practices. These programs often operate on minimum funding and without specially trained teachers. Because these programs are not sponsored under special education law, practice, or finances, they may lack the access to more comprehensive programs that might be suggested by the nature of student characteristics and problems (such as access to mental health services or collaboration with juvenile justice or probation professionals). Given the developmental and experiential complexities that operate in these students' lives, a multidisciplinary, multiagency, coordinated treatment is warranted.

• *Develop clear policies and procedures for school expulsion and support the accuracy of reporting procedures.* Student behavior is fueled by varied circumstances and contexts; consequences should be created with these in mind. Nevertheless, it is important for schools to be able to handle expulsion cases as cleanly and efficiently as possible. This will require that schools have legally sound policies and procedures that protect schools from students' violent behavior and yet afford students the due process protections to which they are entitled (collections of evidence, record keeping, and appropriate conducting of hearings). Implementation of these policies and procedures will require systematic training of key personnel about the procedural and legal foundations of their policies. Legal counsel is not something that all school districts can afford; however, some access to counsel seems cost-effective in terms of the time and energy that is expended on a flawed process that may prevent the desired outcomes.

Local districts and states could benefit from an examination of suspension and expulsion data, disaggregating suspensions from suspension and expulsion incidents. These data could be examined for the overall number of offenses and the number of offenses committed by the same students (the overall number of offenses will include redundant numbers due to the fact that some students are multiple offenders). Data could also be reported by ethnicity, grade, gender, and disability status. An effort should be made to examine these figures on a year-to-year basis and interpret them within the context of the policies and procedures that are operational at the time. An examination of trends for different school administrators would be informative also in order to determine if systematic differences within districts occur with varied administrative practices.

• *Encourage and expand the research interest in expulsion practices and its impacts.* Whether expulsion is used as a public declaration or a more private mechanism to motivate behavior change, there is a desperate need to evaluate its effectiveness. States increasingly are requiring schools to implement research-proven curricula, for example, in academic subjects and in safe and drug-free prevention programs. Zero tolerance is a primary strategy being used to reduce school violence and thus ought to be subject to the same high level of objective research and scrutiny as all other school violence-prevention strategies or programs. Yet, there is no evidence to place zero-tolerance policies and procedures into the "exemplary" or "promising" school violence-prevention categories identified by the

U.S. Office of Education Safe and Drug-Free Schools Office.[45] At a minimum, the short- and long-term consequences of expulsion driven by zero-tolerance policies need to be documented in follow-up investigations.

Conclusion

It is easy to think of zero tolerance as a static event that ends the relationship between the student and the school. In this chapter, we have presented information that suggests that there are complex circumstances before and after the expulsion act that educators and policymakers should consider. Student characteristics and the school's ability to match those characteristics with appropriate educational interventions are important contexts before and after school expulsion. Mismatch between the student and the school system increases the likelihood that students will become involved in expulsion proceedings and that school expulsion as an intervention will be ineffective.

We also considered the complexities of the dual purpose of school expulsion policies: a consequence for individual student rule breaking and a social control message about the outer limits of student misbehavior. This dual purpose poses a conundrum for school officials as they balance the need to treat student behavior with consideration of individual circumstances and the need to maintain safe and orderly school campuses. Future thinking and policy development around school discipline should consider disciplinary action as a complex process that must address the needs of both the students and the school community.

Notes

1. Walker, H. M., Zeller, R. W., Close, D. W., Webber, J., & Gresham, F. (1999). The present unwrapped: Change and challenge in the field of behavioral disorders. *Behavior Disorders, 24*, 293–304.

2. U.S. Department of Education. (1999). *Safe Gun-Free Schools Act Final Report: School year 1997–1998.* [On-line]. Available: www.ed.gov/offices/OESE/SDFS/GFSA/title.html.

3. California Education Code. (Chap. 6, Art. 1, Sec. 48900–48926.

4. U.S. Department of Education, National Center for Education Statistics, & U.S. Department of Justice, Bureau of Justice Statistics. (1999). *Indicators of school crime and safety, 1999*. Washington, DC: U.S. Department of Education.

5. U.S. Department of Education, National Center for Education Statistics, & U.S. Department of Justice, Bureau of Justice Statistics. (1999).

6. Hayden, C. (Ed.). (1996). *Primary school exclusions: A qualitatively different issue?* New York: Routledge.

7. Civil Rights Project. (2000). *Opportunities suspended: The devastating consequences of zero tolerance and school discipline policies.* Cambridge, MA: Harvard University, Advancement Project and the Civil Rights Project. [On-line]. Available: www.law.harvard.edu/civilrights/conferences/zero/zt_report2.html#psych.

8. Brooks, K., Schiraldi, V., & Ziedenberg, J. (1999). *School house hype: Two years later.* Washington, DC: Justice Policy Institute and Children's Law Center. Available: www.cjcj.org/schoolhousehype/shh2.html.

9. Morrison, G. M., D'Incau, B., Couto, E., & Loose, S. (1997). Understanding pathways to student expulsion: Consideration of individual and system indicators. *California School Psychologist, 2,* 53–61.

10. Brooks et al. (1999).

11. Morrison, G. M., & D'Incau, B. (1997). The web of zero-tolerance: Characteristics of students who are recommended for expulsion from school. *Education and Treatment of Children, 20,* 316–335.

12. Morrison & D'Incau. (1997).

13. Hayden. (1996); Morrison & D'Incau. (1997).

14. Civil Rights Project. (2000).

15. U.S. General Accounting Office. (2001). *Student discipline: Individuals with Disabilities Education Act.* (GAO–01–210). Washington, DC: U.S. General Accounting Office.

16. Morrison & D'Incau (1997).

17. Morrison, G. M., & D'Incau, B. (2000). Developmental and service trajectories of students with disabilities recommended for expulsion from school. *Exceptional Children, 66,* 257–272.

18. Individuals with Disabilities Education Act Amendments of 1997, Public Law No. 105–17, 105th Cong., 1st Sess.

19. California Youth Authority. (2001). *Legislature creates California Youth Authority School District.* [On-line]. Available: www.cya.ca.gov/news/cyatoday/sep99/p3a.html.

20. Morrison, G. M., D'Incau, B., Couto, E., & Loose, S. (1997). Understanding pathways to student expulsion: Consideration of individual and system indicators. *California School Psychologist, 2,* 53–61.

21. Morrison et al. (1997).

22. Purkey, S. C., & Smith, M. S. (1983). Effective schools: A review. *Elementary School Journal, 83,* 427–452.

23. Gottfredson, D. G. (1989). *Reducing disorderly behavior in middle schools.* Baltimore, MD: Center for Research on Elementary and Middle Schools. (ERIC Document Reproduction Service No. ED 320 654)

24. Morrison, G. M., Morrison, R. L., & Minjarez, M. E. (1999). *Student*

pathways through school discipline options: System and individual interactions. Paper presented at the 23rd Annual Conference on Severe Behavior Disorders of Children and Youth, Scottsdale, AZ.

25. Civil Rights Project. (2000). p. 15.

26. Zero Tolerance Nightmares. (2001). *Zero tolerance explosion at Bonner Springs High School.* [On-line]. Available: www.ztnightmares.com/html/denise_s_story.htm.

27. Mayer, R. G. (1995). Preventing antisocial behavior in the schools. *Journal of Applied Behavior Analysis, 28,* 467–478.

28. Skiba, R., & Peterson, R. (1999). Zero-tolerance: Can punishment lead to safe schools? *Phi Delta Kappan, 80,* 372–376, 381–382; Townsend, B. (2000). Disproportionate discipline of African American children and youth: Culturally-responsive strategies for reducing school suspensions and expulsions. *Exceptional Children, 66,* 381–391; Brooks et al. (1999).

29. Resnick, M. D., Bearman, P. S., Blum, R. W., Bauman, K. E., Harris, K. M., Jones, J., Tabor, J., Beuhring, T., Sieving, R. E., Shew, M., Ireland, M., Bearinger, L. H., & Udry, J. R. (1997). Protecting adolescents from harm: Findings from the National Longitudinal Study on Adolescent Health. *Journal of the American Medical Association, 278,* 823–832.

30. Ekstrom, R. B., Goertz, M. E., Pollack, J. M., & Rock, D. A. (1986). Who drops out of high school and why? Findings from a national study. *Teachers College Record, 87,* 357–373.

31. DeRidder, L. M. (1991). How suspension and expulsion contribute to dropping out. *Educational Digest, February,* 44–47.

32. Civil Rights Project. (2000).

33. Brooks et al. (1999).

34. Civil Rights Project. (2000).

35. Katsiyannis, A., & Williams, B. (1998). A national survey of state initiative on alternative education. *Remedial and Special Education, 19,* 276–284; Bear, G. G. (1999). *Interim alternative educational settings: Related research and program considerations.* Alexandria, VA: National Association of State Directors of Special Education and U.S. Department of Education, Office of Special Education Programs; Tobin, T., & Sprague, J. (2000). Alternative education strategies: Reducing violence in school and the community. *Journal of Emotional and Behavioral Disorders, 8,* 177–186.

36. *Juvenile justice alternative education program: 1997–1998.* (2001, March, 6). [On-line]. Available: //eric-web.tc.columbia.edu/pathways/expulsion/juvenile.html.

37. *Juvenile justice alternative education program: 1997–1998.* (2001, March, 6).

38. For example, Goss v. Lopez, 419 U.S. 565 (1975).

39. Los Angeles County Office of Education. (2001). *Selected California codes: A compilation of laws related to suspension and expulsion with revisions effective January 1, 2001.* Los Angeles: Division of Student Support Services Attendance and Administrative Services Unit.

40. American Bar Association. (2001). *ABA votes to oppose school zero tolerance policies.* [On-line]: Available: www.abanet.org/media/feb01/zerotolerance.html.

41. Garrison, J. (2001, February 19). Some districts easing rules on discipline. *Los Angeles Times*, pp. A3, A14.

42. Garrison, J., & Elaine G. (2001, March 15). District adopts anti-bullying policy. *Los Angeles Times*, pp. B1, B2.

43. Furlong, M., & Morrison, G. (2000). The school in school violence: Definitions and facts. *Journal of Emotional and Behavioral Disorders, 8,* 71–82.

44. Dwyer, K., & Osher, D. (2000). *Safeguarding our children: An action guide.* Washington, DC: U.S. Departments of Education and Justice. [On-line]. Available: www.air-dc/cccp/guide/annotated.htm.

45. U.S. Department of Education. (2000). *The expert panel on safe, disciplined and drug-free schools searching for best programs.* Washington, DC: Safe and Drug-Free Schools Program. [On-line]. Available: www.ed.gov/offices/OESE/SDFS/programs.html.

GALE M. MORRISON is professor of counseling/clinical/school psychology and special education, risk, and disability studies at the University of California, Santa Barbara.

SUZANNE ANTHONY is a postdoctoral researcher at the University of California, Santa Barbara.

MERI H. STORINO is an assistant professor of school counseling at California State University, Sonoma.

JOANNA J. CHENG is a school psychology intern at the University of California, Santa Barbara.

MICHAEL J. FURLONG is professor of counseling/clinical/school psychology and special education, risk, and disability studies at the University of California, Santa Barbara.

RICHARD L. MORRISON is assistant superintendent of human resources at Ventura Unified School District, Ventura, California.

This chapter examines racial disparities in the application of zero tolerance, describes legal avenues available to parents and children's advocates, and summarizes recent court decisions issued on school discipline cases.

3

Zero tolerance:
Unfair, with little recourse

Judith A. Browne, Daniel J. Losen,
Johanna Wald

FOLLOWING THE PASSAGE of the Gun-Free Schools Act of 1994 by Congress, mandating one-year expulsions of students found in possession of firearms on school property, many state and local school discipline policies extended zero tolerance to a wide range of behaviors.[1] As a result, thousands of students are now routinely excluded from school each year for relatively innocuous or unintentional actions that are neither violent nor dangerous.

Like mandatory sentencing schemes in the criminal law system, zero-tolerance policies were supposed to remove (or at least minimize) discretion and therefore ensure objectivity and the unbiased application of discipline. This is not how these practices were in fact adopted or are implemented. School officials continue to retain discretion in interpretation and application of zero-tolerance

Note: This chapter contains excerpts from *Opportunities Suspended: The Devastating Consequences of Zero Tolerance and School Discipline* (2000), released by Advancement Project and the Civil Rights Project at Harvard University.

NEW DIRECTIONS FOR YOUTH DEVELOPMENT, NO. 92, WINTER 2001 © WILEY PERIODICALS, INC.

policies. Students of color disproportionately receive harsh punishments under zero-tolerance policies, due in large part to the expansion of these policies to cover a range of nonviolent behaviors that are not objectively defined.[2]

As the use of zero-tolerance policies has dramatically increased throughout the country, parents have begun to wage a legal battle to provide clarity in the law and prevent the unfair application of these policies. The results of such legal challenges have been mixed. This chapter examines racial disparities in school discipline, the laws protecting children from discrimination, and current legal challenges to zero-tolerance policies.

Racial disparities and numbers

Racial disparities in the application of school discipline have been documented for over twenty-five years. In 1975, the Children's Defense Fund released *School Suspensions: Are They Helping Children?* a report that revealed that black students were suspended at rates of two to three times that of whites. Black students were also likely to receive longer suspensions and to be suspended more often than whites. Since then, a number of other studies have reported similar patterns.[3]

The widespread use of zero-tolerance policies has exacerbated the racial gap in discipline. In 1998–99, African American students accounted for 33 percent of all those suspended and 31 percent of all those expelled yet made up only 17 percent of all students. According to one recent study, black students are suspended at approximately 2.3 times the rate of whites nationally. Furthermore, black males are disciplined more often and more severely than any other minority group. A 1997 report released by the U.S. Department of Education, *The Condition of Education*, also found that almost 25 percent of all African American male students were suspended at least once over a four-year period. These patterns exist throughout the country. In Maryland, African Americans represent 36 percent of students in that state but 54 percent (34,617) of the state's suspensions. In Massachusetts, minority students constitute only 20 percent of the student population but 54 percent of the state's expelled youth. In Chicago, African American students represented 73 percent of those expelled in 1998–1999, but only 53 percent of student enrollment. In some states with relatively few African American students (Nebraska, Washington, and Iowa), the rate of discipline is between approximately three and four times greater than their proportion in the general student body.[4]

Data obtained in South Carolina for 1998–99 shed further light on this pattern (see Table 3.1). In that state, black children represent only 42 percent of public school enrollment but constitute 61 percent of the children charged with a disciplinary code violation. In addition to representing a disproportionate share of disciplinary actions for some serious offenses, black children in South Carolina were more likely than their white counterparts to be disciplined for such minor acts of misconduct as possession of a pager or disturbing order (by loitering, disturbing peace, or interfering or disturbing in any way with education). Indeed, although black and white children were charged in equal proportions for weapons violations and white students experienced much higher rates of drug charges, the discipline of black students soared in the most subjective categories, where there is greater opportunity for bias or stereotype.

In South Carolina, the consequences for the offense "disturbing schools" (encompassing loitering, disturbing the peace, or interfering or disturbing education in any way), which black children were overwhelmingly charged with, are still serious. Of the

Table 3.1. South Carolina student misconduct, by race

Conduct	Black Students Charged (%)	White Students Charged (%)
Disturbing schools	69	29
Pager	59	40
Weapons	49	49
Drugs	32	65
Assault	71	27
Threatening school official	69	29

Source: South Carolina Public Schools, School Crime Incident Report, 1999.

children charged with disturbing schools, 70 percent were referred to a law enforcement agency, 72 percent were referred for suspension, and 21 percent were referred for expulsion.[5]

The findings of the recent study *The Color of Discipline* are consistent with this pattern. The study found that minority students are disciplined more frequently for subjective offenses, such as loitering or disrespect, than their white peers. These categories of conduct clearly provide more latitude for racial bias to play a part in the use of disciplinary measures. The report suggests that when the data collected in the study are coupled with other data showing racial disparities in school discipline, the disproportionate representation of African Americans in office referrals, suspension, and expulsion is evidence of a "pervasive and systematic bias."[6]

The widespread use of zero-tolerance policies in heavily minority schools must be viewed within a wider context of unequal allocation of resources. Minority students are far more likely than whites to be trapped in high-poverty schools with poorly prepared teachers, unchallenging curriculums, decrepit facilities, and few resources.[7] Counseling staff in their schools are often inadequate. These factors can lead to boredom, disillusionment, and alienation from school, increasing the likelihood that students will engage in conduct teachers may subjectively label disruptive. Yet these are the very behaviors that can most easily be remedied through measures that do not require exclusion from school.[8]

Impact of harsh punishment on minority children

Many psychologists and educators suggest that harsh punishment, particularly if it is perceived as unfair, often backfires and ends up exacerbating behaviors it was meant to remedy. Two of the nation's leading African American child psychiatrists, James P. Comer and Alvin F. Poussaint, have written, "When punishment is necessary, it should not be harsh and traumatic for minor incidents. . . . [Overly harsh punishment] either destroys a child's spirit, has no effect at all, worsens the problem, or makes it more difficult . . . to work with the child in school—he or she no longer trusts you."

Furthermore, there is some evidence that when minority groups are singled out for particularly harsh treatment, the result is even more deleterious. Brenda Townsend, associate professor of special education at the University of South Florida, argues that when the majority of school suspensions and expulsions are meted out to a minority of the school population, those students are likely to interpret the disparity as rejection and as a result develop a collective self-fulfilling belief that they are incapable of abiding by schools' social and behavioral codes. Susan Black, an education research consultant, notes that "these kids often interpret suspension as a one-way ticket out of school—a message of rejection that alienates them from ever returning to school." This may explain recurring suspensions of students and the correlation between dropout rates and suspensions and expulsions.[9]

Overreliance on suspensions and expulsions may adversely affect adolescent behavior. In fact, adolescents may view suspensions and expulsions as unfair and unreasonable. Such a reaction may be exacerbated where minority students unfairly bear the overwhelming brunt of disciplinary actions. The unreasonable, and sometimes absurd, application of zero-tolerance policies has resulted in a backlash through numerous court challenges.

Challenging zero-tolerance policies

Students subjected to discriminatory and unfair zero-tolerance policies and practices do not shed their rights at the schoolhouse doors. Federal and state law protections include protections against discrimination on the basis of color or national origin, free speech protections as defined in the First Amendment, constitutional due process protections, protections for students with disabilities, and state laws providing rights to a public education. In many cases, multiple legal claims are warranted.

Although these legal protections, as interpreted by courts, provide an incomplete patchwork of legal protections against the imposition of harsh school disciplinary measures, the tide may be changing. Courts typically give broad deference to school officials regarding matters of school governance, including school discipline. Thus, the outcome of court challenges has been mixed. However, a few courts, perhaps responding to the apparent increase of harsh sanctions for innocuous conduct, have started to give the laws that are protective of students' rights more teeth. Moreover, the American Bar Association (ABA) recently passed a resolution against the use of zero-tolerance policies in schools, which may add to courts' discomfort with the more egregious examples of these practices. In its policy statement, the ABA writes that "zero tolerance has become a one size fits all solution to all the problems that schools confront. It has redefined students as criminals, with unfortunate results."[10]

While federal laws provide general civil rights protections that may extend to the school environment, state laws specifically address school discipline issues. Beyond banning firearms and other weapons from school grounds, state laws have provided the impetus for increasing suspensions and expulsions for nonviolent conduct. State laws permit or require suspension or expulsion of children for conduct such as disruptive behavior, willful defiance of authority, or gross disobedience. In some instances, profanity is enough to warrant removal from school.[11] Parents who believe that their children have been unfairly caught up in the zero-tolerance craze have sought to limit the expanse of zero-tolerance policies and lessen ambiguities in the laws and policies. Although some courts have questioned the efficacy of zero-tolerance policies and practices, judges are often bound by legal precedent in school discipline cases that have allowed limits on free expression and not required extensive due process.

Protections against discrimination

The evidence suggests that these unnecessarily harsh discipline policies not only raise issues of fundamental fairness, but their implementation may often violate the civil rights of children of color. Civil rights are always violated when the discriminatory effect is intentional but can also be implicated when unsound educational policy unintentionally burdens minority students more than white students.

Fourteenth Amendment. The equal protection clause of the Fourteenth Amendment to the U.S. Constitution prohibits discrimination on the basis of race, color, or national origin. This provision of the Constitution applies to all public school systems. However, obtaining such equal protection under the law may be difficult because the burden of proof is quite onerous. The Supreme Court has held that only intentional discrimination violates the Equal Protection Clause.

Although data and anecdotal evidence suggest that intentional discrimination may be widespread, proving it is likely difficult in most school discipline situations. For example, one key point in the disciplinary process where discrimination might occur is the initial decision to refer a student for discipline. Data show that students of color are more likely than whites to be referred for subjective infractions such as showing disrespect. A challenge under constitutional law would have to establish that white children who were referred for the same behavior got more favorable disciplinary treatment. Because many white students are not referred for disciplinary action, the task of proving that students of color were treated differently from similarly situated white students may be very difficult. However, discrimination may be inferred where large racial disparities in discipline, combined with other evidence of discrimination, suggest a systemic pattern or practice of differential treatment.[12]

Although proving intentional discrimination may be difficult, some school districts have been found to have violated the Fourteenth Amendment, typically for maintaining segregated schools. Disciplinary practices in such school districts may be subjected to careful review. School districts under school desegregation orders are required to eliminate the vestiges of their prior dual systems. Thus, discriminatory disciplinary actions in such a district may violate an existing court order. The case of *Bronson* v. *Board of Education of Cincinnati* is perhaps the best example.[13] In *Bronson*, the Court reviewed a 1991 study that revealed that racial disparities had not changed since the original desegregation consent decree entered in 1984.[14] Moreover, suspension and expulsion rates had risen dramatically following the implementation of a new policy that added the use of profanity toward staff as grounds for suspension.[15] As a result of the ongoing disparities, the consent decree was amended to require that schools monitor teachers' discipline referrals and intervene when referral rates were high and show substantial racial disparity. Interventions included positive incentives for teachers who demonstrated competence in behavior management, as well as the potential of job loss for those who failed to improve their classroom management skills after having been provided with opportunities to do so.

School desegregation cases present significant opportunities to eliminate racially discriminatory disciplinary practices. In the context of ongoing court supervision, discriminatory disciplinary practices may be challenged and may gain a presumption of intentional discrimination because of the failure to eliminate the vestiges of discrimination.

Administrative Enforcement of Title VI of the Civil Rights Act of 1964. Title VI prohibits discrimination on the basis of race, color, or national origin in federally funded programs. Thus, it applies to any school system receiving federal financial assistance, which means virtually all public schools.

Federal investigators from the Department of Education's Office for Civil Rights (OCR) are not limited by the evidentiary standard requiring proof of intent that a court would apply.[16] Title VI regulations promulgated by the U.S. Department of Education *do* permit a finding of discrimination based on statistical evidence of a racially adverse and "disparate impact," without requiring proof of intent.

Under the disparate impact theory, when a racially neutral policy or practice produces a disproportionately harmful impact on students of color, the burden shifts to the school system to justify its policy or practice. At least two rationales support this approach. First, by focusing on consequences instead of intent, the theory scrutinizes practices that may result from intentional discrimination, even when that intent is impossible to detect or prove. Forcing the defendant to justify its practices ensures that its actions are based on clearly legitimate reasons and are not a subterfuge for undetectable intentional discrimination. Second, given the history of racial exclusion in the United States, the disparate impact theory represents a policy decision, repeatedly reaffirmed by Congress, that regardless of intent, actions that pile additional disadvantages on historically oppressed groups should not be permitted unless supported by a compelling justification.[17]

The less onerous burden of proof available under the disparate impact theory, which is embodied in the Department of Education's regulations, was potentially powerful protection in discipline cases until the Supreme Court recently limited its reach. In *Alexander* v. *Sandoval*, the Supreme Court rejected the argument that there was an implied "private right of action" available to individuals to enforce the Title VI disparate impact regulations in court.[18] The *Sandoval* ruling does not preclude individuals, or organizations, from seeking the enforcement of the disparate impact regulations but leaves enforcement authority in the hands of the OCR.[19]

If it were vigorously enforced, the disparate impact standard under Title VI could be a potent tool for challenging disciplinary systems that produce large racial disparities. Once a complainant proves such a disparity, the school must show that the practice is "educationally justifiable." Under this standard, a defendant school district must show that the goals of fostering a safe and orderly learning environment are actually served by the policy in question. In addition, even if the school system meets its burden, the complainant can prevail by showing that an alternative approach to discipline would achieve these goals with a less discriminatory impact.[20] These standards, "educationally justifiable" and "less discriminatory alternative," should make it very difficult for any school system with significant racial disparities to justify a harsh system of discipline.

Furthermore, because few cases lead to full-scale litigation, OCR may work toward a change in policy where statistical evidence is suggestive of intentional discrimination. In most cases, OCR focuses on identifying and resolving potential violations through negotiated resolutions followed by monitoring for compliance. As a result, many complaints are settled without a formal agency determination on the legal claim.

A review of OCR's resolution agreements and other documents, conducted by the Civil Rights Project at Harvard, indicates that OCR typically processes race-based school discipline complaints and compliance reviews with an emphasis on finding intentional discrimination instead of relying on statistical disparate impact. Although OCR does use statistical analysis to determine which districts to investigate, the documents suggest that once begun in full, the investigation usually focuses on finding evidence of intentional discrimination. Where none was found, the agency often did not continue to investigate in order to complete the disparate impact analysis. Specifically, where OCR analyzed racial disparities in discipline involving categories of subjective offenses, the educational necessity of such discipline or alternatives with less discriminatory alternatives was not examined.[21] Moreover, OCR's tendency to investigate and resolve complaints without publicizing the results fails to send warning signals that school systems with egregious racial disparities in discipline need to reconsider their policies and practices.

The disparate impact standard under Title VI may nudge school systems toward employing less punitive and more educationally sound models of discipline. In 1996, OCR acted on a complaint filed against a high school in Alameda, California. Without explicitly citing the disparate impact standard, OCR pointed to a significantly higher rate of discipline against Latino and African American students, particularly in the area of "disrespect of authority." The agency negotiated with the school district to implement conflict resolution teams, peer counseling groups, workshops addressing issues of race, and a retreat for administrative staff that covered racial stereotyping, profiling, and communication styles. Particular attention was paid to discipline for defiance of authority. These steps led to a steep decline in both the overall suspension rates and racial disparities in disciplinary referrals. OCR did not close the case until these improvements had been documented, but questions remain regarding the comprehensiveness of OCR monitoring in such cases.

The Alameda case illustrates the potential of OCR's Title VI enforcement authority to produce measurable outcomes that advance racial justice and benefit both students and schools. Unfortunately, the lack of clear and accessible information about OCR investigations, resolution agreements, and monitoring efforts and outcomes diminishes the potential for any ripple effect for the agency's enforcement efforts. Clear messages must be sent to schools that racial disparities in disciplinary actions raise the specter of discrimination and that school districts must take steps to eliminate these disparities so as to ensure that no one group of students is singled out or left behind.

Title VI has great potential for curing the adverse effects of disciplinary actions on minority students. However, as a result of recent Supreme Court jurisprudence, the promise of Title VI may lie solely in the hands of the Department of Education. Thus, strong enforcement by the Department of Education is now more important than ever before.

First Amendment protections

First Amendment challenges to school discipline have typically involved students punished for profanity or alleged threats. These cases assert that students' actions were protected under the free speech clause.

Challenges to zero-tolerance policies under the First Amendment have been unsuccessful in many recent cases due to interpretations of legal precedent that have increasingly limited the First Amendment rights of students. While students do not "shed their constitutional rights to freedom of speech or expression at the schoolhouse gate," their rights "are not automatically coextensive with the rights of adults in other settings." In fact, a school may limit speech of students that is "inconsistent with its pedagogical mission, even though the government could not suppress that speech outside of the schoolhouse." Students are permitted to express personal views unless it is determined that such expression will substantially disrupt the classroom. Ultimately, the determination of what manner of speech is appropriate lies, for the most part, with school officials, not courts.[22]

Zero-tolerance policies banning profanity have been upheld as constitutional despite the First Amendment's speech protections. In South Dakota, a student who discovered that he would have to take the bus home and noticed that the buses had already left blurted out an expletive. As a result, he received a two-and-one-half-day suspension. His parents challenged the disciplinary action in court on First Amendment grounds. Although the federal court expressed some disconcert with the school's action, stating that the student's conduct was not disruptive to the educational environment or to others in the school and it was "perhaps too much to do about relatively little," it held that the school had power to regulate indecent language in an effort to promote decency and civility.[23]

First Amendment challenges to zero-tolerance policies have also arisen where school officials have claimed that students' expression constituted threats to safety or harassment. Courts have concurred that the First Amendment does not protect threats, but they have differed in determining what expression is threatening. A twelve-year-old Massachusetts student who drew a violent scene in which he shot his teacher was suspended for three days and adjudicated as delinquent. The Massachusetts Supreme Court held that in the light of highly publicized incidents of school violence, which the court detailed in its opinion, the drawing constituted a threat for which no constitutional protection would ensue. Similarly, a Wisconsin Court of Appeals concluded that a student's creative writing assignment describing how a teacher had kicked a student out of class and was later killed by the same student could be considered a direct threat of violence, and thus was not protected speech.[24]

Courts have differing opinions about what constitutes free speech in the school setting. In a similar case, a federal court in Oklahoma protected a student's speech despite its threatening nature. An Oklahoma high school student was suspended for writing a poem that mentioned killing a teacher, in violation of the school's zero-tolerance policy that prohibited threats. School officials admitted that the student's poem was not a genuine threat and was not intended to instill fear in the teacher. Unlike the Massachusetts Supreme Court, the Oklahoma District Court found it "impossible to have a 'no tolerance' policy against 'threats' if the threats involve speech because a student cannot be penalized for what they are thinking." The Oklahoma court ordered the student's return to school. In fact, the Supreme Court has stated that an "undifferentiated fear or apprehension of disturbance is not enough to overcome the right of freedom of expression" for public school students.[25]

The First Amendment's application to zero-tolerance policies has also arisen in the case of a policy against racial harassment and intimidation. In Kansas, a seventh-grade student was suspended for drawing a Confederate flag on a piece of paper. The school found that this conduct violated its zero-tolerance policy banning racial harassment and intimidation that had been adopted in response to racial tensions at the school. The Tenth Circuit Court of Appeals held that the school's action did not violate the student's First Amendment rights. It stated that while the same conduct by the student would have been protected if he were outside the school, the school could limit such speech if it would be disruptive. In the light of racial hostility at the school, the court found that the school appropriately regulated the student's speech.[26]

First Amendment protections afforded students are not as expansive as those that are extended outside educational settings. The limitations of such protections are highly contextualized determinations, ultimately left to courts to decide.

Due process protections

The constitutionality of zero-tolerance policies has also been questioned under the due process clause of the Fourteenth Amendment to the Constitution. This clause, which applies to the states and their subdivisions, provides real but limited protections to students subjected to harsh school discipline. Due process has two distinct components. The first, procedural due process, requires states and their local governmental subdivisions to provide fair and adequate notice and procedures prior to depriving a person of liberty or property interests. For example, although there is no federal guarantee of a public education, when states choose to provide it, courts have determined that there is a property interest in a free public education.[27] Therefore, depriving a student of an education for more than ten days on disciplinary grounds could violate the due process clause. The second aspect of the due process clause, substantive due process, is concerned with whether a state may impair a given "fundamental right" or whether the procedures employed violate principles of "fundamental fairness." Thus, disciplinary actions may not be "arbitrary and capricious" or "grossly disproportionate" to the offense. Despite the tendency of courts to defer to school officials in applying the rationality standard of substantive due process, lawyers and activists are considering strategies to convince courts to put more teeth into the substantive due process rationality review.

The procedural element of due process governs issues such as the type of hearing required before an adverse action can be taken, whether there is a right to counsel, and the evidence that can be considered. The procedures required prior to suspending a student for ten or fewer days are informal and minimal. However, more formal procedures and greater rights accrue when a longer suspension or expulsion is at issue. Due process entitles students facing suspension to, "at the very minimum . . . some kind of notice and afforded some kind of hearing" before a punishment is imposed.[28] These cases are regularly litigated and typically question whether a district complied with its hearing procedures.

Because there is no judicially recognized right to an education under the U.S. Constitution, review and revision of a school suspension on substantive due process would be available only in a rare case where there was no "rational relationship between the punishment and the offense."[29] When substantive due process is at issue, the state must have a compelling interest to justify its actions, which must be narrowly tailored to achieve that interest. Due process challenges to zero-tolerance policies and practices have met mixed results.

Typically, courts leave disciplinary actions to the discretion of school officials. The highly publicized case of four teenagers in Decatur, Illinois, expelled for fighting was ultimately brought before a federal court in Illinois. In reviewing the claims of substantive due process violations, the court reiterated long-standing law that limits court involvement in school discipline matters: "It is not the role of the federal courts to set aside decisions of school administrators which the court may view as lacking a basis in wisdom or compassion." Furthermore, the court, recognizing that education is not a fundamental right, stated that disciplinary policies are constitutional unless they are "wholly arbitrary" and thus failing rational basis. The court also reviewed claims of violations of the students' procedural due process rights, which requires that the student know of the charges, receive notice of the expulsion hearing, and is given an opportunity to explain his position in an evidentiary hearing. The court held that the district complied with all due process requirements.[30]

Although courts have deferred to school authorities and afforded them broad discretion in fashioning punishments, disciplinary decisions must be rational and the circumstances of each situation must be considered. A federal court of appeals found that the application of a zero-tolerance policy was irrationally applied in a Tennessee district's decision to expel a student for possession of a weapon where the student was unaware of the presence of a weapon. The school district asserted that intent to harm is not required by its zero-tolerance policy. However, the court stated, "No student can use a weapon to injure another person, to disrupt school operations, or . . . for any other purpose if the student is totally unaware of its presence." The application of the policy was held to be irrational and thus in violation of due process.[31]

Consideration of extenuating circumstances and students' disciplinary records can be critical, especially in cases where the

student's infraction was unintentional (for example, students who
find weapons and take steps to prevent their use or students who
drive a parent's car to school not realizing a weapon is in the glove
box or trunk);[32] whether individual circumstances are considered
can mean the difference between a long-term expulsion and minimal punishment. In *Colvin* v. *Lowndes County*, the court considered
the case of a sixth-grade boy who was expelled under an unwritten
zero-tolerance policy for inadvertently bringing a Swiss Army knife
to school even though he threatened no one with the item and
turned it over to his teacher without incident. The court noted that
while a recent violent incident in Pearl, Mississippi, prompted additional local efforts to eliminate school violence, "such efforts must
be balanced with the constitutional guarantees afforded to the children that enter the schoolhouse door." The court berated the
school district's "manner in which it blindly meted out the student's
punishment." Ultimately, the court reversed the school district's
decision to expel the student, ordering it to reconsider without
applying a "blanket policy of expulsion." The court held that due
process requires the use of independent consideration of relevant
facts and circumstances.[33]

In some cases, procedural due process also requires the hearing
and disciplinary decision to include an individualized consideration
regarding the appropriate punishment. Although the due process
clause does not prevent school boards from adopting and applying
mandatory punishments, it does require individualized treatment
when state law or school board policy allows for case-by-case determinations or modification of mandatory penalties. In these situations, which are common across the fifty states, school boards may
not simply defer to a written or unwritten zero-tolerance policy or
to the recommendation of other school officials such as the principal. Instead, as part of making an independent disciplinary decision, the school board (or the equivalent decision-making body)
must consider the nature of the offense; the student's age, record,
and past behavior; and any mitigating factors. Further, although
the Gun-Free Schools Act does require expulsion for at least one

year for any student found bringing a firearm to school, it also mandates a procedure allowing case-by-case review by the chief administrative officer for the district. State laws therefore must grant local school officials the same discretion. Moreover, nothing in the federal law limits the state or local district from providing alternative educational services to an expelled student.

Due process challenges to zero-tolerance policies do present some opportunity to challenge the discretion of school officials to mete out punishments. These protections will likely be used more often to combat unfair disciplinary practices.

Legal rights of students with special needs

Federal law provides a plethora of protections for children with special needs that could serve as valuable safeguards for them. The enforcement of these laws falls within the jurisdiction of numerous state and federal agencies. These laws are highly complex, with varying administrative schemes and differing procedural rules on questions such as exhaustion of administrative remedies. Because one of the most potent legal requirements in this area strictly prohibits imposition of discipline when a student's disability contributed to the alleged misconduct, one might expect the level of discipline against students with special needs to mirror that of the general student population. However, the much higher levels of discipline for these students raises concern about the extent to which school districts are complying with these laws.[34]

Three federal statutes provide basic protections for students with disabilities. The Individuals with Disabilities in Education Act (IDEA) is specifically targeted toward students with disabilities and their families, and the Americans with Disabilities Act of 1990 and the Rehabilitation Act of 1973 prohibit discrimination against persons with disabilities, including students.

IDEA provides the most comprehensive set of rights for students with disabilities. The overarching principle of this law mandates that school systems provide a free and appropriate public education to all children with disabilities in the least restrictive environment. Each state has adopted laws and regulations to implement IDEA and must maintain a mechanism for resolution through administrative hearings.

Although students with disabilities can be held to most generally applicable standards of conduct and subjected to discipline, disabilities may contribute to students' actions. If a student's misconduct is caused by a disability or if the school district has failed to provide appropriate services and supports to students, the district's authority to impose suspension or expulsion is narrowed. Nonetheless, none of these limitations prevents a principal from removing a student with disabilities from school immediately if that student poses an imminent threat of physical harm to self or others. IDEA also allows for an expedited hearing for longer-term removal from school where the school authorities argue that a student continues to pose an imminent threat of physical harm to self or others. Many of the procedural rights and restrictions on removal are also modified under federal law when possession of weapons or drugs is at issue.

When the failure of the school to provide appropriate services to the student is not at issue and the student's misconduct is not caused by his or her disability, the general disciplinary sanction, including suspension or expulsion, may be imposed on a student with a disability. However, even in this situation, IDEA provides students with disabilities with a right not available to all students: a free and appropriate public education. Thus, school districts must continue to provide such students a comprehensive education with the services the student needs in the least restrictive setting and to the maximum extent appropriate. Moreover, removal from school for more than ten days triggers the school's obligation to conduct a functional behavioral assessment, if one has not been performed recently, to ensure that if the student needs behavioral supports and services, they will be met appropriately, wherever the student continues to receive educational services.

The determination of whether the student's misconduct was caused by a disability is critical under IDEA. For any suspension longer than ten consecutive days, the school system must hold a "manifestation hearing" to determine whether the triggering misconduct was a manifestation of the student's disability. The act provides important procedural safeguards and substantive protections, and favorable court precedents make this law valuable to students and parents with access to good legal advice or representation. Unfortunately, it appears that many special needs students do not have access to attorneys with expertise in this complex area of law and that school systems often do not fully comply with these IDEA provisions.[35]

Despite evidence that suggests that students with special needs are not receiving preferential treatment with regard to discipline, politicians often assert that an unfair double standard is applied to students with disabilities. In 1997, the General Accounting Office was commissioned by Congress to study this claim. In January 2001, after surveying hundreds of school principals across the nation, it concluded that "special education students who are involved in serious misconduct are disciplined in generally a similar manner to regular education students."[36] Nonetheless, some elected officials continue to press for amendments to IDEA to deprive students with disabilities entitlement to continuing education if they are suspended or expelled.

In addition to requiring manifestation hearings and continued education, systemic challenges to a system of discipline that violates the rights of special needs students as a class can be effective in some situations. Such systemic violations of IDEA might include assignment of all children with emotional disorders to special classrooms or a pattern of failing to diagnose students with disabilities and provide them with the legally required services and protections.

Under disability laws, even unintentional violations can be sufficient grounds for allegations of unlawful discrimination. Most important, the failure to provide a free and appropriate public education in the least restrictive environment may form the basis of discrimination claims under Title II of the Americans with Disabilities Act or Section 504 of the Rehabilitation Act of 1973. Regulations pursuant to Section 504 also provide protections against disciplinary practices with a disproportionate adverse impact on students with disabilities that generally mirror the disparate impact standard applied under Title VI. In addition, IDEA regulations require record keeping and monitoring of the racial impact of the identification and placement of students with disabilities, including long-term suspensions, expulsions, and the placement of students with disabilities into alternative schools.

Finally, given the increased routing of students into the criminal justice system, it is noteworthy that IDEA has been held to limit a school system's ability to initiate proceedings against students with disabilities that could lead to incarceration. For example, in *Morgan* v. *Chris L.*, a federal court of appeals held that a school had violated IDEA by failing to evaluate a student with attention deficit hyperactivity disorder in a timely manner and attempting to use the juvenile court process to change his educational placement without following proper IDEA procedures. The court ruled that the school's filing of a delinquency petition against the student for allegedly damaging a water pipe in a school bathroom constituted a change in educational placement that entitled the student to IDEA protections, including the meeting of the Individualized Education Program team prior to the proposed placement change.[37]

IDEA and other disability laws provide a basis for protecting students with special needs from disciplinary actions taken in response to conduct related to a disability. In effect, these laws should be an equalizer for children with special needs to ensure that they are not unfairly punished for behavior they could not control. These laws provide procedural protections for children to ensure that the disciplinary process itself is fair. In addition, the laws require that these children not be penalized for conduct by refusing them an opportunity to learn. The protections outlined in these laws should serve as a model for rights that other children should be afforded.

Students' rights to a public education

Although the U.S. Supreme Court has concluded that there is no fundamental right to an education that originates in the U.S. Constitution, state constitutions "may be the most important source of protection for expelled and suspended students." In some states, "the highest courts have declared the right to education to be fundamental and deserving of strict analysis for equal protection purposes." For example, children in California, Connecticut, New Jersey, and Pennsylvania have a fundamental right to an education.[38]

In 2000 in New Jersey, the fundamental right to an education was upheld in the context of a zero-tolerance expulsion. A fifteen-year-old student, along with several other students, was charged with making a false public alarm and expelled for allegedly making a false bomb threat call to his school. This conduct violated the school's zero-tolerance policy, which required expulsion of students involved in making bomb threats. The school not only expelled the student but also refused to provide any educational alternatives for him. The court concluded that the state had the constitutional obligation to provide the student with an education, even though he had been placed on probation and had been expelled by the local school district. The state was directed to provide the student with an alternative school program until he either received his high school diploma or turned age nineteen.[39]

Although an alternative school placement is preferable to no educational opportunity at all, it raises serious concerns for a number of reasons. Anecdotal evidence indicates that many alternative school programs do not provide students with an adequate education. These schools are often found to have watered-down curriculum and poorly trained or unqualified teachers. For example, in 1999, the superintendent for Palm Beach County, Florida, entered into a resolution agreement with OCR to address a race- and disability-based complaint regarding the district's use of alternative education programs. After further investigation, OCR found "significant disproportion" by race in the number of African American students involved in incidents where law enforcement became involved and significant disparities in the rate of disciplinary referrals and punishment of African American students for a wide range of offenses.[40]

Furthermore, the idea of isolating at-risk children is generally regarded as a recipe for failure and distinctly frowned on in the area of special education research and law. Systemic challenges sounding in both Title VI and disability law may be effective in curtailing the inappropriate use of these alternative programs.[41]

Some politicians nevertheless appear willing to commit large numbers of poor and minority children to these experimental institutions. For example, some members of the Illinois legislature have proposed legislation to permit schools to transfer at-risk children to alternative schools. This broad category "may include without limitation" students who are economically disadvantaged, involved in substance abuse, have attendance problems, or are involved with the police or courts. The proposed legislation explicitly allows districts to contract with programs operated by the Department of Corrections.[42] This proposal raises grave concerns about student isolation, labeling of students, academic tracking, and inadequate academic opportunities for students.

Other court challenges to zero tolerance

Zero-tolerance policies have been contested on various other grounds in recent years. For example, in Georgia, a high school student was adjudicated delinquent for possession of a knife on school grounds. The student possessed an art or craft knife with a blade less than three inches long. The court reversed the adjudication because the art knife did not fall within the definition of a knife under the state's law prohibiting weapons on campus. Courts have also struck down expulsions under zero-tolerance policies where there was insufficient evidence to charge a student with a particular violation.[43]

Conclusion

Incidents of sweeping and mindless applications of zero-tolerance policies continue to make national headlines.[44] Despite the media attention and even widespread ridicule that such stories evoke, there is no indication that zero-tolerance policies are abating. In fact, recent proposals to require school safety programs to identify and exclude "disruptive" children are almost certain to increase racial profiling of children and exacerbate racial disparities in discipline. For example, legislation proposed in Mississippi would require automatic expulsion of students found disruptive on three or more occasions in a school year. Other states may follow suit. Litigation over such laws will surely ensue in an effort to protect the constitutional and civil rights of students. It is uncertain how such suits will fare in courts. Although in the past, many have been reluctant to challenge the authority of schools to mete out discipline as they see fit, even courts have occasionally bristled at the severity and irrationality of these disciplinary codes. Yet stronger legal protections for students are needed.

As a group of outraged New Jersey parents illustrated recently, an organized and strategic effort mounted at the school district level may be a more expedient way to reverse irrational and harmful zero-tolerance policies than time-consuming litigation. While strategic legal action remains an important avenue for parents and advocates to pursue, they might be well advised to do so in concert with other public education, lobbying, and organizing efforts.

Notes

1. 20 U.S.C. §§ 8921–8923 (1994). The law required states to pass laws to comply or face loss of federal funding. The Gun-Free Schools Act permits school administrators to forgo expulsion of students found with firearms on school property depending on the circumstances. Many schools have also extended harsh punishments to behaviors that are subjectively defined, such as disrespect, disobedience, and disorderly conduct.

2. Thornton, C. H., & Trent, W. T. (1998). School desegregation and suspension in East Baton Rouge Parish: A preliminary report. *Journal of Negro Education, 57*, 482; McFadden A. C., Marsh G. E., Price B., & Hwang Y., (1992). A study of race and gender bias in the punishment of handicapped children. *Urban Review, 24*, 239; Kids First Coalition. (1999). *Locked out: Exposing the suspension epidemic in the Oakland Public Schools*. Oakland, CA: Kids First Coalition.

3. Children's Defense Fund. (1975). *School suspensions—Are they helping children?* Cambridge, MA: Washington Research Project, Children's Defense Fund. See generally Skiba, R. J., Michael, R., Nardo, A., & Peterson, R. (2000). *The color of discipline: Gender and racial disparities in school punishment*. Bloomington, IN: Indiana Education Policy Center.

4. Smith, T. M. (1997). *The condition of education 1997*. Washington, DC: U.S. Department of Education, Office of Educational Research and Improvement; U.S. Department of Education, Office of Civil Rights. (2000, August).

Fall 1998 Elementary and Secondary School Civil Rights Compliance Report, Projections. Washington, DC: Author. Several studies and statistical reports detail racial disparities in school disciplinary actions. U.S. Department of Education, Office for Civil Rights. (1997). *1997 Elementary and secondary school civil rights compliance report.* Washington, DC: U.S. Department of Education; Johnston, R. (2000). Federal data highlight disparities in discipline. *Education Week,* June 21, 2000; Brooks, K., Schiraldi, V., & Ziedenberg, J. (2000). *Schoolhouse hype: Two years later.* Washington, DC: Justice Policy Institute and Children's Law Center; Gordon, R., Piana, L. D., & Keleher, T. (1999). *Making the grade: A racial justice report card.* Oakland, CA: Author; Generation Y. (2000). *Suspended education: A preliminary report of the impact of zero tolerance on Chicago Public Schools.* Chicago: Southwest Youth Collaborative.

5. South Carolina Public Schools. (1999). *School crime incident report.* Columbia, SC: South Carolina Public Schools.

6. Skiba et al. (2000).

7. Lee, J. W. (1998). Giving kids a chance: An outstanding responsive teacher in every classroom. New York: Conference on high stakes testing, Dec. 4, 1998.

8. We interviewed several principals about their policies and philosophies regarding school discipline. Even the brightest students, one principal explained, get in trouble when they are bored. Inexperienced teachers are far more likely than those with more classroom experience and training to rely on excluding students to control their classroom. One principal who routinely suspended large numbers of students conceded that good teachers do not experience chronic disciplinary problems and that teachers could benefit from more training in managing their classrooms. Advancement Project and the Civil Rights Project at Harvard University. (2000). *Opportunities suspended: The devastating consequences of zero tolerance and school discipline.* Cambridge, MA: Author.

9. Comer J. P., & Poussaint A. F. (1992). *Raising black children.* New York: Penguin Books. pp. 197–198; Townsend, B. The disproportionate discipline of African-American learners: Reducing school suspensions and exclusions. *Exceptional Children, 66,* 381–391; Black, S. (1999). Locked out: Why suspension and expulsion should be your court of last resort. *American School Board Journal, 186,* 34–37. DeRidder, L. M. (1991). How suspension and expulsion contribute to dropping out. *Education Digest, 56,* 44–51.

10. American Bar Association, Criminal Justice Section. (2001). *Zero tolerance report.* Chicago: Author.

11. For a discussion regarding state zero-tolerance laws, see Advancement Project and the Civil Rights Project at Harvard University. (2000).

12. In re Benedictin Military School, Individuals With Disabilities Education Law Report, 22, 643 (1995) (OCR finding discipline policy to violate Title VI based on the fact that black students were routinely expelled from the school at the headmaster's discretion, but white students were rarely, if ever, suspended or expelled for similar or even graver offenses).

13. Bronson v. Board of Education of Cincinnati, No. C-1-74-205, Amended Consent Decree (Doc. #840) (S.D. Ohio 1994).

14. Bronson *v.* Board of Education of Cincinnati 604 F.Supp. 68 (S.D. Ohio 1984).

15. Schmidt, P. (1993). Cincinnati agreement will rate teachers on discipline. *Education Week*, November 10, 1993.

16. See 34 C.F.R. 100.3(b)(2). U.S. Department of Education, Office of Civil Rights. (2000). *The use of tests when making high-stakes decisions for students: A resource guide for educators and policymakers.* Washington, DC: Author. Guardians Association *v.* Civil Service Commission, 463 U.S. 582, 589–590 (1983) (holding that the Title VI regulations forbid the use of federal funds "not only in programs that intentionally discriminate on racial grounds but also in those endeavors that have a[n] [unjustified racially disproportionate] impact on racial minorities").

17. For further discussion about Title VI enforcement, see U.S. Commission on Civil Rights. (1996). Equal Educational Opportunity Project Series (Vol. 1, pp. 156–157). Washington, DC: U.S. Government Printing Office.

18. The Court did not address the validity of the disparate impact regulations themselves: "We must assume for purposes of deciding this case that regulations promulgated under § 602 of Title VI may validly proscribe activities that have a disparate impact on racial groups, even though such activities are permissible under § 601." Sandoval, 121 S. Ct., at 1513.

19. The private right of action under Title VI regulations may still be available through 42 U.S.C. § 1983, which prohibits state action that deprives a citizen of his or her rights. For more on this issue, see Sandoval, 121 S. Ct. 1511, at 1527; Access Living of Metropolitan Chicago *v.* Chicago Transit Authority, 2001 WL 492473 (N.D. Ill.); Mank, B. C. (2001). Using § 1983 to enforce Title VI's section 602 regulations. *University of Kansas Law Review, 49,* 321; Powell *v.* Ridge, 189 F.3d 387, 400–403 (3d Cir. 1999). It remains to be seen how severely the Court's holding will curtail the ability of private parties to bring actions in court against state actors to enforce the Title VI disparate impact regulations. But see South Camden Citizens in Action *v.* New Jersey Department of Environmental Protection, 2001 WL 1602144 (3rd Cir. N.J.) (holding that § 1983 does not allow plaintiffs to invoke Title VI disparate impact regulations in a private action in court).

20. Less discriminatory alternatives are discussed further in In the Matter of Dillon County School District No. 1, Lake View South Carolina, 1987 Education Civil Rights Reviewing Authority LEXIS 12 (April 17, 1987) (in holding a school tracking practice to be unlawful, the review board stated, "If the employer, or in this case, the District, has less onerous or less discriminatory alternatives that it could use, then its failure to do so is a pretext for discrimination").

21. See San Lorenzo (CA) Unified School District, *Individuals with Disabilities Education Law Report, 33,* 252, June 2000 (complaint raised issue that minority students were disproportionately disciplined among other claims; resolution agreement included OCR continued monitoring for disparities in discipline); Paducah (KY) Independent Schools, *Individuals with Disabilities Education Law Report, 32,* 182, October 1999 (class allegations, among others, regarded disproportionate discipline by race; decision in favor of parent states

that resolution agreement will include monitoring for compliance, but attached agreement lists no details with respect to monitoring for disproportionate discipline by race).

22. Anderson v. Milbank School District 25–4, 197 F.R.D. 682, 685–88, (D. S.D. 2000) (citations omitted). D.G. v. Independent School District No. 11 of Tulsa City, Oklahoma, 2000 U.S. District LEXIS 12197 (N.D. OK Aug. 21, 2000).

23. Anderson, 197 F.R.D. at 686–688.

24. Commonwealth v. Milo M., 433 Mass. 149 (2001). In the interest of Douglas D., No. 99–1767-FT, 2000 WI App. 32, at *7–8 (Wisc. Ct. App. Dec. 14, 1999).

25. D.G. v. Independent School District No. 11 of Tulsa County, Oklahoma, 2000 U.S. District LEXIS 12197; Tinker v. Des Moines Independent Community School District, 393 U.S. 503 at 508 (1969).

26. West v. Derby Unified School District 260, 206 F.3d 1358, 1361–1364 (10th Cir. 2000).

27. For example, see Goss v. Lopez, 419 U.S. 565 (1975).

28. Goss v. Lopez, 419 U.S. 565 (1975).

29. Brewer v. Austin Independent School District, 799 F.2d 260, 264 (5th Cir. 1985).

30. Fuller v. Decatur Public School Board of Education School District 61, 78 F. Supp. 2d 812 (C.D. Ill., 2000) (quoting Woodland v. Strickland, 420 U.S. 308, 326 (1975)).

31. Seal v. Knox County Board of Education, 229 F.3d 567 (6th Cir. 2000).

32. Examples of unintentional violations of zero-tolerance policies appear in Lyons v. Penn Hills School District, 723 A.2d 1073 (Pa. Commw. 1999); Enterprise City Board of Education V.C.P., 698 So. 2d 131 (Ala. Civ. App. 1996).

33. Colvin v. Lowndes, No. 99V306, 2000 U.S. District LEXIS 2403 (N.D. Miss. Feb. 24, 2000). Similarly, in Lyons v. Penn Hills School District, 723 A.2d 1073 (1999), a state court in Pennsylvania struck down a zero-tolerance policy on weapons because it denied the superintendent discretion to modify punishments under the policy.

34. For a comprehensive discussion of the rights of students with disabilities and disparities in discipline, see Ordover, E. (2000). Disciplinary exclusion of students with disabilities. Brooks et al. (2000).

35. Polakow–Suransky, S. (1999). *Access denied: Mandatory expulsion requirements and the erosion of educational opportunity in Michigan.* Ann Arbor: Student Advocacy Center of Michigan.

36. U.S. General Accounting Office. (2001). *Student discipline: Individuals with Disabilities Education Act.* Washington, DC: U.S. General Accounting Office.

37. Morgan v. Chris L., 106 F.3d 401 (6th Cir. 1997) (affirmed). 1997 WL 22714 (6th Cir. Tenn.).

38. Cerrone, K. M. (1999). The Gun-Free Schools Act of 1994: Zero tolerance takes aim at procedural due process. *Pace Law Review, 20,* 131; Reed, R. R. (1996). Education and the state constitutions: Alternatives for suspended

and expelled students. *Cornell Law Review, 81,* 582; Bartholomew v. Hamden Board of Education, 1996 Conn. Super. LEXIS 2534, *3; State ex rel. G.S., 330 N.J. Super. 383, 393 (N.J. Super. Ct. Ch. Div. 2000).

39. State ex rel. G.S., 330 N.J. Super. at 393–394. In Tennessee, a student found in possession of a weapon on school property was expelled without alternative education for violating the school's zero-tolerance policy. The court held that Tennessee state law leaves alternative school assignments to the discretion of school officials. Davidson v. Wright, 1997 Tenn. App. LEXIS 398 (1997).

40. The complainant had previously won a Commissioner's Order (Agency Case Number DOE-98-344-FOF), which included a corrective action plan developed jointly among the complainant, district administrators, and bureau staff issued on December 2, 1998. Despite this agreement, another complaint was filed against the district alleging similar violations. This complaint resulted in a new resolution agreement, Palm Beach County School District, #04–99–1285 (September 7, 2000).

41. See 20 U.S.C. § 1400 et seq.; Individuals with Disabilities Education Act Amendments of 1997. Congressional findings acknowledge substantial concerns about restrictive and segregated classrooms and conclude that isolated students are usually worse off compared to similarly situated mainstreamed students. 20 U.S.C. § 1401(C)(4) (5).

42. House Bill 1096, An Act concerning alternative learning opportunities (2001). State of Illinois 92nd General Assembly Legislation.

43. In re R.B.W., 98 FCDR 1710 (S. Ct. GA 1998). Crawley v. School Board of Pinellas County, FL, 721 So. 2d 396, 397 (Fla. District Ct. App. 1998); D.R. v. State of Indiana, 729 N.E.2d 597, 599–600 (Ind. App. 2nd District 2000).

44. Zernicke, K. (2001, May 17). Crackdown on threats in schools fails a test. *New York Times;* Danielson, R. (2001, March 10). Zero tolerance leaves zero options. *St. Petersburg Times;* Judgment takes recess in Cobb School. (2000, September 29). *Atlanta Journal Constitution.*

JUDITH A. BROWNE is senior attorney at the Advancement Project, a public policy and legal action organization that advances universal opportunity and a racially just democracy. The Advancement Project has offices in Washington, D.C., and Los Angeles.

DANIEL J. LOSEN is legal and advocacy associate for the Civil Rights Project at Harvard University, a think tank that addresses the racial justice dimensions of key public policy issues.

JOHANNA WALD is the research coordinator and writer-editor for the Civil Rights Project at Harvard University.

A number of programs with empirical evidence of effectiveness in addressing problems of aggression and disruption have emerged in schools.

4

Alternative strategies for school violence prevention

Joseph C. Gagnon, Peter E. Leone

TRAGIC SCHOOL SHOOTINGS of children by children have caused parents, teachers, principals, and community members throughout the nation to question their basic assumptions about school safety. Schools should be nurturing environments promoting children's intellectual and social development, but disruptions that interfere with learning can create a climate of fear in which children avoid school or engage in self-protective behavior. Although shootings with multiple victims represent an extreme example of school violence, these rare incidents have shaped much of the discussion about how to prevent violence and create safe schools.[1]

Many segments of the public believe that school violence is increasing. The most current data on school violence and youth victimization in the United States indicate, however, that schools are the safest places for children and that serious acts of violence have decreased since 1993.[2] Fewer homicides and violent crimes are committed against children at school than in their homes or on the streets. In fact, students are more than forty times more likely to be the victim of a homicide away from school than at school. Most injuries that children experience at school are not violence

NEW DIRECTIONS FOR YOUTH DEVELOPMENT, NO. 92, WINTER 2001 © WILEY PERIODICALS, INC.

related, and the majority of school crime is theft, not assault. Finally, data reported by the Federal Bureau of Investigation as part of the Uniform Crime Reports, as well as students' self-report of victimization in the National Crime Victimization Surveys, indicate that violence perpetrated by and against youth continues to decline.

Assessing the effects of violence-prevention efforts

Measuring the efficacy of violence-prevention efforts is difficult. The conceptualization and definition of school violence shape how schools respond to the problem and measure prevention efforts.[3] Depending on the definition of the term, acts of school violence can range from threats of physical violence, to bullying, physical assaults, and homicide.

Assessing the impact of violence-prevention efforts requires data on the current level of school violence. Many of the data are based on student and teacher perceptions of school safety, official police reports, and telephone interviews of adolescents.[4] Data-gathering methods to assess school violence vary considerably, and perceived violence is consistently reported at higher levels than self-reports of violent incidents.[5] This is due, in part, to media reports of school violence. For example, following the highly publicized shootings at Columbine High School in 1999, public perceptions of the safety of schools deteriorated markedly.[6] Reports of school safety are also highly dependent on the group interested in studying the problem. School administrators and school boards may not be interested in tallying and publicizing all acts of school crime and disorder. Historically, school administrators have underreported and handled serious acts of misconduct at school informally. In contrast, parents and community groups may find this same information vital to their support of schools and school leadership. In recent years, mandatory reporting requirements associated with the Drug Free and Safe Schools Act have required greater disclosure by the schools.

Violence prevention in context

Dramatic changes in public schools during the past decade have affected the ways in which schools respond to violence and disruption. Among these changes are an increased focus on accountability, information technology, and achievement in the public schools. Accountability and an emphasis on literacy for the information age have created a greater sense of urgency among educators. Teachers, principals, and superintendents are being asked to measure and demonstrate tangible academic gains in student performance.

As academic expectations have increased, there has been a decrease in school tolerance for deviant behavior. In this high-stakes climate, disruptive students, particularly those who score poorly on tests that measure the performance of the classroom, school, or school district, are at risk for being excluded from the education community. Zero-tolerance policies nominally have been created to provide better opportunities for other students to achieve academic milestones by removing so-called troublemakers from the school. By removing low-achieving disruptive students from the schools, these policies may increase the likelihood that average levels of student achievement will rise in order to meet state or district standards.

Effective practice

Zero-tolerance school policies have led to a more punitive approach to student behavior,[7] focusing on a limited number of reactive and punitive responses to problem behavior, including office discipline referrals, in- and out-of-school suspension, and expulsion. Although these approaches may be perceived as providing immediate and short-term relief to teachers and administrators, they fail to address the school structures and processes necessary for effective prevention of serious misconduct (see Chapters One and Two, this issue).

Fortunately, researchers and practitioners have identified and assessed the efficacy of more positive and proactive approaches to violence prevention. These interventions can be placed in three categories: schoolwide or universal interventions, student-centered approaches, and school security measures. In the following sections, we examine empirically validated and promising programs, schoolwide and student-centered interventions, and school security measures.

Universal interventions

Schoolwide or universal interventions attempt to create school and classroom climates for all children that promote social and academic growth and a sense of community. These interventions endeavor to create a culture within the school in which respect for the individual, predictability, and the perception of fair play shape the behavior of teachers, students, and administrators.

Effective universal or schoolwide behavioral support relies on development and implementation of a systematic approach to training, monitoring, and reinforcement of appropriate behavior.[8] These interventions may exist as a component of a comprehensive schoolwide plan that addresses universal and individualized interventions or as a more general program that attends solely to schoolwide interventions. For example, the Resolving Conflict Creatively Program (RCCP) focuses solely on a schoolwide educational program that teaches and reinforces appropriate social skills for all students (although the RCCP is currently developing a component of the program that targets high-risk students). The other two schoolwide interventions programs, Project ACHIEVE and Positive Behavioral Interventions and Supports (PBIS), also include plans for targeting small groups of at-risk students and individual interventions for youth who do not respond to more general interventions.

Resolving Conflict Creatively Program

This K-12 school-based intervention supports youth in the development of social and emotional skills necessary to decrease violence and prejudice, form relationships, and develop healthy lives.[9] RCCP is an example of a social-cognitive intervention in which students are taught conflict resolution through modeling, role playing, interviewing, and small group work. The fifty-one weekly lessons are used to teach skills such as communication, listening, self-expression, dealing with anger, conflict resolution, cooperation, recognizing the value of diversity, and countering bias.

Training is an essential component of the RCCP program. Teachers receive training and ongoing support to facilitate their integration of concepts and skills into the existing curriculum. In addition, school administrators, support staff, and parents receive training in conflict resolution techniques consistent with those imparted to teachers. A select group of students receive peer mediation training.

A comprehensive review of research revealed that the social-cognitive approach used within RCCP was effective for all age groups of students in reducing crime, antisocial behavior, and conduct problems.[10] Specifically related to RCCP, results were promising when the teachers received a moderate amount of training and assistance, covered half of the lessons or more, and had a low number of peer mediators in their class.[11] Students in these classes were significantly less hostile. Furthermore, student prosocial behavior increased, as compared to students in classrooms where teachers taught fewer RCCP lessons and relied on relatively more peer mediators. Although the empirical support for peer mediation as an effective strategy in isolation is inconsistent, it may be more effective when included as part of a multicomponent intervention such as RCCP. In addition, because there were fewer positive effects for boys, younger children, and children in high-risk classrooms and neighborhoods, supplementing RCCP with other effective interventions is advisable.

Project ACHIEVE

Project ACHIEVE, a universal intervention for elementary and middle schools, provides training to school personnel in six areas: problem solving, social skills and behavior management, effective teaching and instruction, curriculum-based assessment and academic interventions, parent education and training, and organizational planning, development, and evaluation. Preliminary evaluations of Project ACHIEVE are promising. Positive effects include a 28 percent decrease in discipline referrals and a 6 percent decrease in out-of-school suspensions. In addition, after three years, the suspension rate decreased from 11 percent to 3 percent.[12]

Implementing Project ACHIEVE requires an initial analysis of school strengths and needs and a schoolwide functional behavioral assessment. This assessment includes an analysis of current discipline procedures; student, teacher, and environmental characteristics and issues; and available resources. The information obtained from the assessment provides the basis for intervention planning. In addition, the Project ACHIEVE model includes processes for developing general hypotheses, collecting data, developing and implementing the intervention, and evaluating the effectiveness of the intervention based on the data.[13]

Project ACHIEVE has strong parent and teacher training components. The goal of both is for students to be consistently exposed to and use identified social skills and procedures for dealing with conflict across a variety of settings. The parent training program provides instruction in effective tutoring, positive behavior management, and information on their child's curriculum. Parents are provided opportunities to use this information within organized classroom tutoring of their own and other children. Consultants also assist parents in implementing these approaches at home.

Project ACHIEVE components target high-risk students and others who require individualized interventions. Specifically, teachers are trained to use data from curriculum-based measures to identify students who are at risk for failure or are achieving below expectations. Based on the contexts in which these students experience academic or behavioral difficulties, teachers implement specific instructional adaptations and behavioral supports. Such adaptations or interventions can be implemented with individuals or small groups of students who are experiencing difficulties. For example, if a student or group of students has difficulty with homework, the teacher assesses the context of the student behavior to identify if direct instruction of a specific skill would be appropriate or if students possess the needed skills and implementation of a behavioral intervention is appropriate. Consultants provide support to teachers with record keeping and data analysis to help assess the effectiveness of the intervention.

Positive Behavioral Interventions and Supports

PBIS, another universal prevention program, is designed for all students and includes setting (such as playground and lunchroom) and classroom-specific support for students who have chronic behavior problems.[14] Results of the PBIS model are promising, with a reduction in office referrals ranging from 30 percent to 68 percent. Furthermore, these results have been maintained over several years with continued implementation. To maintain positive results, ongoing staff commitment and access to technical assistance and consultation from an outside source (a university) are important, as well as regular leadership team meetings to review data on office discipline referrals, identify behavioral patterns, and make data-driven decisions related to program modification.[15]

As with Project ACHIEVE, an initial step in this process is to identify issues unique to the school through a functional behavioral assessment. With the agreement and support of the principal and at least 80 percent of the staff, a building-based team is formed. This team is responsible for the "development, implementation, modification, and evaluation of prevention efforts"[16] and bases its decisions on six central components of the PBIS model:

(a) an agreed upon and common approach to discipline; (b) a positively stated statement of purpose; (c) a small number of positively stated expectations for all students and staff; (d) procedures for teaching these expectations to all students; (e) a continuum of procedures for encouraging displays and maintenance of these expectations: (f) a continuum of procedures for displays of rule-violating behavior; and (g) procedures for monitoring and evaluating the effectiveness of the discipline system on a regular and frequent basis.[17]

Effective universal interventions

Promising results exist for comprehensive prevention programs that focus on universal interventions and also address the needs of individual students with more serious behavior. RCCP, Project ACHIEVE, and PBIS are based in part on the belief that school discipline consists of more than establishing and enforcing rules by reacting to inappropriate student behavior.[18] Five critical components exist within the effective universal interventions discussed: (1) schoolwide functional behavioral assessment or needs assessment and intervention planning; (2) teacher, administrator, and parent support and education; (3) clear rules, consequences, and conflict resolution and skills training for students; (4) effective instruction; and (5) ongoing monitoring of student behavior and outcomes.

As an initial step in developing a violence-prevention program, RCCP, Project ACHIEVE, and PBIS include a form of schoolwide needs assessment and intervention planning. Understanding the context in which behaviors occur provides the foundation for planning and implementing an appropriate program. In addition, Project ACHIEVE and PBIS rely on a team-based approach to problem identification and implementation of interventions. The Project ACHIEVE model uses four teams: (1) a multidisciplinary school staff team to complete the initial needs assessment; (2) a master teacher and classroom teacher team, whereby the master teacher provides an instructional model and slowly fades his or her role in the classroom; (3) grade-level teams; and (4) a schoolwide discipline committee comprising the grade-level team leaders. Within the PBIS model, the leadership team consists of teachers, the principal, a parent, and another member of the school staff.

The team is expected to "conduct instructional or environmental analysis, collect and analyze data, develop academic or social skills lessons, and develop and make accommodations to specialized academic or behavioral support plans."[19]

These universal programs consistently address the issues of teacher, administrator, and parent support and education. For example, Project ACHIEVE and PBIS identify teacher participation in the prevention interventions as critical. Although the RCCP program does not set a specific rate of teacher acceptance prior to implementation, the authors acknowledge the importance of teacher investment in the program. Once commitment to program implementation is acquired, continued support and education are provided. Within the PBIS and RCCP models, outside consultants provide training and ongoing support. Existing staff provide the training and consultation within Project ACHIEVE. Also, all three programs advocate parent participation. Of particular note is Project ACHIEVE, which includes both involvement and training of parents and school support staff (for example, paraprofessionals, custodians, and bus drivers).

Training and support of educators is accompanied by a school-wide focus on clear rules and consequences, and conflict resolution and skills training for students. This focus is significant, given that youth violence has been linked to a lack of social and problem-solving skills.[20] Experts agree that skills training is an effective alternative to suspension and sends an appropriate message to students that they are wanted in school. In addition to teaching skills for negotiating nonviolent outcomes to conflict, youth are instructed in interpreting social cues and taking the perspective of others. Project ACHIEVE and PBIS also emphasize the importance of effective instruction as part of universal interventions. Within Project ACHIEVE, teachers are trained and supervised in curriculum analysis, use of curriculum-based measures, and implementation of empirically validated instructional practices. Although no specific component within PBIS addresses effective instruction, the program has been integrated into a schoolwide literacy model. In addition, interventions such as direct instruction, use of manipulatives, peer collaboration, and other empirically validated instructional practices have been included within the PBIS model.[21]

Another important component that Project ACHIEVE, PBIS, and RCCP share is the ongoing monitoring of student behavior and outcomes. Among the indicators used to identify student progress are incidence of office discipline referrals, suspension rates, student achievement, and special education referral and placement. The use of empirical evidence accurately identifies students who require individual as well as universal interventions.

Targeted approaches

This second group of interventions seeks to change the behavior and school experiences for specific students. Targeted interventions may provide special programs, classes, or schools for those who have engaged in specific acts of misconduct or those most at risk for engaging in antisocial and disruptive behavior. Interventions aimed at individual students or groups of students can also teach specific skills such as conflict resolution strategies or social skills.

Student-centered approaches focus on the 5 to 10 percent of the student population who are at risk for disciplinary problems. These students require additional support beyond universal, schoolwide plans.[22] Schools must detect students at risk and identify those with chronic behavior problems in order to provide appropriate and effective interventions. Here we look at two central topics: the early identification and detection of students and examples of two effective student-centered approaches: Positive Adolescent Choices Training (PACT) and First Step to Success.

Early identification and early detection

Implementing individual student intervention begins by identifying students who do not respond to universal interventions. Estimates are that approximately 40 percent of student discipline referrals are given to 5 percent of the student population.[23] Consequently, reviewing office referrals may be a method for identifying students who require additional interventions. At-risk students might also be identified through analysis of attendance data, juvenile justice involvement, and direct observation. This process of establishing which students are not benefiting from universal intervention is referred to as early identification.

In contrast, early detection can be used prior to student misconduct and focuses on students who are at a high risk for violent and antisocial behavior. One effective tool for early detection is the Systematic Screening for Behavior Disorders.[24] This instrument, which provides a multiple-step procedure for detecting students at risk, includes an initial teacher referral process based on a review of the behavior of every student in the classroom. Students are then ranked based on adaptive and maladaptive behavior and observation. Early detection is distinct from early identification in that detection requires a systematic screening to recognize the students who are at high risk. In contrast, early identification is an individual prevention process that considers which students have already experienced difficulties. Both approaches provide an effective system of assessing students and deciding who may benefit from an intervention beyond the schoolwide plan.

Early detection and identification are not simply steps toward the identification of students in need of special education.[25] Rather, they are processes through which students can receive the supports they need to maintain positive social interactions.

Positive Adolescent Choices Training (PACT)

The PACT program, a cognitive-behavioral intervention designed to be sensitive to the cultural needs of adolescent African American students who are at risk for violence, has helped to reduce physical aggression and adjudication for participating students.[26] The focus is on modeling appropriate behavior and instruction in problem-solving strategies and includes role playing and videotaped vignettes that portray African Americans modeling specific skills. PACT is designed to provide participants with skills to resist violence and negotiate conflicts, such as giving and receiving positive and negative feedback, resisting peer pressure, and problem solving. Students are taught methods for expressing difficult feelings (anger, frustration, disappointment, and others) and appropriate means of resolving conflicts. A third component of PACT, anger management, deals with recognition of anger, self-control, and consideration of consequences to actions, and is designed to help students understand the consequences of serious misconduct.

First Step to Success

The First Step to Success program is a student-centered approach designed for students in kindergarten who exhibit aggressive or defiant behavior. The program has shown significant positive effects for aggression, academic engagement time, adaptive, and maladaptive behavior that have been maintained over time.[27] The program uses skills training and a reward system to teach and reinforce positive student behavior. Following an initial identification process, consultants work with teachers, parents, and students to coordinate a program across school and home settings. The school program consists of a system of awarding students points at regular intervals for appropriate behavior. The home component includes a child skills program with lessons on five topics: self-expression, developing self-confidence, cooperation, solving problems, and interacting with others. Students are reinforced for positive school behavior at both school and home.

Effective targeted interventions

Targeted interventions for violence prevention are those designed for small groups of at-risk students or students who have been identified as not benefiting from universal interventions. The PACT and First Step to Success programs provide a snapshot of effective interventions for small groups of students. Several commonalities exist between these two examples and the research on effective interventions for students requiring support beyond universal interventions. For example, both include components of cognitive-behavioral and social-cognitive strategies, approaches that have consistently resulted in positive student outcomes. Specifically, both programs include instructing students on methods for solving problems, self-expression, and interacting positively with others.

Intensive interventions

Universal interventions and programs, such as PACT and First Step to Success, target small groups of students and may have a positive impact on a majority of students. However, individual behavioral interventions are necessary for 3 to 5 percent of the student population for whom inappropriate behavior has become a persistent problem. Two approaches that show some promise in meeting the needs of these students are the use of functional behavioral assessment and alternative educational programs.

Functional behavioral assessment

Functional behavioral assessment (FBA) is a process through which a problem behavior is identified and clearly described. Direct observation and interviewing establish the contexts in which a behavior occurs and the consequences that maintain the behavior.[28] Based on this information, individualized interventions can be implemented. For students receiving special education services, the use of FBA is required by the Individuals with Disabilities Education Act when school personnel take actions that remove students for more than ten days from their educational placement. Although this is an effective use of FBA, to limit its implementation to purposes of reaction reduces its possible benefits in the prevention of student violence.

FBA has great potential as a proactive strategy. For example, it is effective for nondisabled students and can be effectively blended with common classroom interventions.[29] The PBIS model integrates the use of FBA into the development of programs at the universal and individual student levels. Extended training for all teachers and a team-based approach to implementation may be necessary for widespread and effective use of FBA. A review of current research revealed that a validated FBA methodology does not currently exist; however, procedural similarities do exist across forms of FBA. Further research is needed to delineate specific procedures for effective use of this approach.

Alternative schools

A primary guide to the effectiveness of alternative programs is their ability to provide student participation in the general education curriculum and, when appropriate, with support services and modifications.[30] However, the tremendous variability in student composition, structure, and purpose makes it difficult to develop any generalized statement on the effectiveness of these programs. For example, alternative placements include schools within schools, punitive alternative placements that substitute for suspension or expulsion, continuation schools that students attend voluntarily after leaving the public schools, schools within the juvenile justice system, and charter schools. In spite of this variability, alternative programs do appear to have a small but positive effect on student academic performance, attitude, and self-esteem.[31] Furthermore, alternative schools that serve a specific target population tend to have a more significant effect on these variables. Two major concerns with the alternative schools research exist, however: problems with the quality of the studies (lack of a control group, random sampling, and follow-up when students return to regular public schools) and lack of positive effects noted on the delinquent behavior of participants.

Because alternative schools are an option that many schools employ, an examination of alternative settings and identification of the common components associated with program success is justified. Clearly, elements of effective intervention at either the universal and individual student level are relevant to effective violence prevention in alternative settings. In addition, a number of crucial components to effective alternative placements have been identified:

(a) procedures for conducting functional assessments of the skills and learning needs of the students; (b) a flexible curriculum that teaches functional academics, social and daily living skills; (c) effective and efficient instructional techniques; (d) transitional programs and procedures that tie the alternative school to the public school and to the community; (e) comprehensive systems for providing both internal alternative school services and external community services to students; and (f) availability of appropriate staff and resources for students with disabilities.[32]

Identification of critical characteristics for effective alternative programs is a positive starting point. Additional research is necessary, however, to develop specific strategies and maximize the benefit of alternative settings for students related to academic achievement, serious misconduct, and attitude toward school.

Effective intensive interventions

Intensive interventions provide another level of support for students who do not benefit from universal interventions or those that target small groups of students. Although there is less empirical validation of alternative schools and functional behavior assessment, individualization for students with severe and chronic behavior problems and the analysis of the contexts in which behaviors are exhibited seems a promising approach.

School security measures

Implementing school security measures is another popular strategy in the effort to prevent violence. This group of interventions is designed to detect and deter potential perpetrators of school violence before they harm themselves or others. The use of metal detectors, school security officers or school resource officers, and surveillance cameras are all examples of school security measures that have been introduced to prevent school violence. In contrast to universal interventions and efforts focused on specific individuals, these measures introduce into school settings techniques that are frequently associated with the anonymous control of individuals in airports and prisons.

In 1999, the Office of Justice Programs of the U.S. Department of Justice issued a report, *The Appropriate Use of Security Technologies in U.S. Schools*.[33] While acknowledging that school security measures are not the answer to all problems associated with violence in the schools, the document makes an explicit assumption that security technology, such as surveillance cameras and metal detectors, is an important component of a school security plan.

Unfortunately, although many school districts have purchased hardware to detect weapons that could be brought into school buildings, there is little evidence that these measures create safer education environments. A statewide study in California reported that most school districts used violence-prevention curricula and had strong police and security. In addition, schools reported using surveillance cameras, canine searches, and metal detectors. But the majority of school districts had no evidence supporting the effectiveness of these efforts.[34] An ethnographic study of efforts to suppress gang activity in three urban high schools examined the effectiveness of metal detectors, surveillance cameras, perimeter fencing, and school security officers. The evidence suggested that these measures were ineffective in suppressing gang activity and student violence in the schools.[35]

An analysis of responses from over nine thousand youth from the 1995 National Crime Victimization Survey examined students' perception of school violence and disorder in schools with secure buildings (that is, places that emphasized security measures like metal detectors, locked doors, and personal searches), and schools with a system of law (that is, schools where the rules were emphasized and the consequences of breaking the rules were known). Findings suggest that when students know the rules and consequences for misbehavior and are aware that the rules in a school are applied fairly under the system of law, less victimization and disorder is present in the school. Where disorder exists, students reported engaging in more acts of self-protection. In contrast, the more efforts taken to run a secure building through physical means (metal detectors) and personnel interventions (school resource officers, staff watching hallways), the more victimization and disorder (fights, thefts) were reported present, and the less safe students reported feeling.[36]

Identifying successful approaches

Table 4.1 provides examples of the three approaches to violence prevention and compares the results of research in each of the areas. This analysis of alternative strategies for school violence prevention identified several features of successful approaches. Schools that effectively prevent serious misconduct have "policies (e.g., proactive discipline handbooks, procedural handbooks), structures (e.g., behavioral support teams), and routines (e.g., opportunities for students to learn expected behavior, staff development, data-based decision making) that promote the identification, adoption, implementation, and monitoring of research-validated practices [emphasis added]."[37] Finally, the link between academic achievement and student behavior is clearly documented in the research.[38] Together, these results indicate that the goal of violence-prevention programs should be broadly conceived to include controlling student behavior and supporting student academic success.

Several research-based recommendations for effective violence prevention in schools flow from our review of literature:

Policies

- Clear rules and consequences: Clearly stated rules and consequences for students, teachers, and administrators are important components of effective universal interventions. The positive effects on student behavior when teachers establish, teach, and reinforce rules have been well documented.

Structures

- Principal support: Administrative support is critical for successful prevention programs. Evidence suggests that support should be visible, predictable, and continuous.

Table 4.1. Responses to school violence and disruption

Intervention	Type of Response	Examples	Staff Training	Empirical Support	Staff Time Required	School Climate and Culture
Universal, schoolwide interventions	Proactive, preventive	RCCP, Project ACHIEVE, PBIS	Yes, initial training, on-going support	Yes	All staff: Initial investment of time, on-going involvement	Positive changes
Student-centered approaches	Reactive, preventive	Project ACHIEVE, PBIS, PACT, First Step to Success	Yes, on-going	Yes	Small group of staff: Initial investment of time, on-going involvement	No changes
School security measure	Reactive, preventive	Surveillance cameras, metal detectors, security officers	No	No	Outside staff: On-going involvement	Potential negative changes

- Ongoing support to staff: Continuing access to qualified consultants can assist educators in their attempts to implement procedures with a high level of fidelity.
- Parent and community involvement across settings: Positive results are obtained through extending school-based prevention programs to a number of domains of student life. Parents, and other community members whenever possible or appropriate, are important in supporting prevention programs.

Routines

- Needs assessment and functional behavioral assessment: The needs and available resources of the school must be evaluated. Furthermore, an assessment of the needs and values within the community, school, teachers, and student contexts can be used to develop procedures and interventions that are socially and culturally appropriate.
- Staff acceptance: Staff willingness to support and implement a program is critical to its success. Students show significantly more improvement with teachers who implement a prevention program consistently.
- Staff training: Critical components of a prevention plan can be appropriately implemented and maintained through comprehensive staff development.
- Conflict resolution and social skills training for students: Programs focusing on conflict resolution and social skills training frequently use direct instruction, teacher and peer modeling, role playing, and rehearsal to teach students. Programs focusing on these aspects have consistently resulted in reduced inappropriate behavior, increased student attendance, and short-term gains in problem solving, particularly for younger and disadvantaged children. Results of a recent meta-analysis indicate that social skills training in isolation may have limited effects on students with emotional and behavioral disorders.[39] However, combining schoolwide social skills training and targeted group behavioral interventions has been successful in reducing inappropriate student behavior in the lunchroom, on the playground, and during hallway transitions.

- Program monitoring and effective implementation: Consistent and high-quality program implementation is essential. The quality of program implementation may be more important than whether a program was implemented. Quality prevention programs are increasingly using student outcome data (office discipline referrals, suspension rates, student achievement and special education referral and placement) to monitor program effectiveness.

Conclusion

Approaches to violence prevention based on zero tolerance of proscribed behaviors and removal of students from school settings are at best short-term solutions. Youth suspended or expelled from school because of threats or acts of violence may need to be removed from school for short periods of time. Yet long-term suspensions and expulsions merely transfer school problems to the community. Without assistance and support, youth who need behavioral interventions and quality education programs become prime candidates for the agency of last resort: the juvenile justice system. Evidence suggests that the effective strategies to reduce school violence involve schoolwide strategies such as RCCP, Project ACHIEVE, and PBIS. There is also evidence that individually targeted interventions such as conflict resolution and social skills instruction, systematic classroom management, parent involvement, early warning and screening, and implementing individual behavior plans are promising strategies for reducing school violence.

Schools should consider several principles when planning violence-prevention initiatives. First, schoolwide violence-prevention initiatives based on a public health model are effective. Schoolwide interventions by design systematically address the needs of all students, including those with significant academic, emotional, or behavioral problems. These approaches typically include more intensive interventions for students with severe academic and social needs. Second, although the use of security technology may be politically popular and may convince the public that administrators are addressing threats to the safety of the school, there is no evidence supporting the effectiveness of these approaches in preventing school violence and some evidence that the use of security technology may actually exacerbate school disorder. Third, effective schoolwide prevention initiatives are comprehensive and multicomponent and provide a broad range of services and supports over a sufficient period of time. Because the antecedents of youth violence are highly correlated, prevention programs that address a range of interrelated risk and protective factors have greater potential than single-focus programs.

Notes

1. Sheley, J. F. (2000). Controlling violence: What schools are doing. In S. G. Kellam, R. Prinz, & J. F. Sheley (Eds.), *Preventing school violence: Plenary papers of the 1999 Conference on Criminal Justice Research and Evaluation—Enhancing Policy and Practice Through Research* (Vol. 2, pp. 37–57). Washington, DC: US Department of Justice, National Institute of Justice.

2. For information on trends in youth crime, see Brenner, N. D., Simon, T. R., Krug, E. G., & Lowry, R. (1999). Recent trends in violence-related behaviors among high school students in the United States. *Journal of the American Medical Association, 282*(5), 440–446; Brooks, K., Schiraldi, V., & Ziedenberg, J. (2000). *School house hype: Two years later.* Washington, DC: Justice Policy Institute; Kauffman, P., Chen, X., Choy, S. P., Chandler, K. A., Chapman, C. D., Rand, M. R., & Ringel, C. *Indicators of school crime and safety 1998.* (Publication NCES 1998–251/NCJ-172215). Washington, DC: 1998; Rand, M. (1998). *Criminal victimization 1997: Changes 1996–97 with trends 1993–97.* Washington, DC: US Department of Justice, Bureau of Justice Statistics; U.S. Department of Education. (1999a). *Annual report on school safety.* Washington, DC: Author.

3. For a discussion of the problems associated with defining and conceptualizing school violence, see Furlong, M., & Morrison, G. (2000). The school in school violence: Definitions and facts. *Journal of Emotional and Behavioral Disorders, 8,* 71–82.

4. Louis Harris and Associates. (1999). *The Metropolitan Life survey of the American teacher, 1999.* New York: Author; U.S. Department of Justice and Federal Bureau of Investigation. (2000). *Crime in the United States: Uniform crime reports, 1999.* Washington, DC: Author; U.S. Department of Justice, Bureau of Justice Statistics. (1998). *National crime survey: School crime supplement, 1998.* Washington, DC: Author.

5. Furlong, M., & Morrison, G. (1994). Introduction to miniseries: School violence and safety in perspective. *School Psychology Review, 23*(2), 139–150.

6. Brooks et al. (2000).

7. See Gottfredson, G. D., Gottfredson, D. C., Czeh, E. R., Cantor, D., Crosse, S. B., & Hantman, I. (2000). *National study of delinquency prevention in schools.* Ellicott City, MD: Gottfredson Associates; Nelson, C., Scott, T., & Polsgrove, L. (1999). *Perspectives on emotional/behavioral disorders: Assumptions and their implications for education and treatment.* Reston, VA: Council for Exceptional Children.

8. Sugai, G., Sprague, J. R., Horner, R. H., & Walker, H. M. (2000). Preventing school violence: The use of office discipline referrals to assess and monitor schoolwide discipline interventions. *Journal of Emotional and Behavioral Disorders, 8,* 94–101.

9. About the Resolving Conflict Creatively Program. [On-line]. Available: www.esrnational.org/about-rccp.html; Thornton, T. N., Craft, C. A., Dahlberg, L. L., Lynch, B. S. & Baer, K. (Eds.). (2000). *Best practices of youth violence prevention: A sourcebook for community action.* Atlanta, GA: Centers for Disease Control and Prevention, National Center for Injury Prevention and Control.

10. Gottfredson et al. (2000).

11. See Aber, J. L., Brown, J. L., & Henrich, C. C. (1999). *Teaching conflict resolution: An effective school-based approach to violence prevention.* New York: National Center for Children in Poverty; Brooks et al. (2000).

12. Knoff, H. M. (1999). *Project ACHIEVE: Project overview and focus on creating a building-based social skills, discipline/behavior management, and school safety system.* [On-line]. Available: www.coedu.usf.edu/projectachieve/; Knoff, H. M., & Batsche, G. M. (1995). Project ACHIEVE: Analyzing a school reform process for at-risk and underachieving students. *School Psychology Review, 24,* 579–603.

13. Sugai, G., Horner, R. H., Dunlap, G., Heineman, M., Lewis, T. J., Nelson, C. M., Scott, T., Liaupsin, C., Sailor, W., Turnbull, A. P., Turnbull, H. R., Wickham, D., Reuf, M., & Wilcox, B. (2000). Applying positive behavioral supports and functional behavioral assessments in schools. *Journal of Positive Behavior Intervention, 2*(3), 1–23.

14. For information on the PBIS model, see Dwyer, K., & Osher, D. (2000). *Safeguarding our children: An action guide.* Washington, DC: U.S. Department of Education; Lohrmann-O'Rourke, S., Knoster, T., Sabatine, K., Smith, D., Horvath, B., & Llewellyn, G. (2000). Schoolwide application of positive behavior support in the Bangor area school district. *Journal of Positive Behavioral Support, 2*(4) [On-line]. Available: www.pbis.org/english/index.html; Taylor-Greene, S. J., & Kartub, D. T. (2000). Durable implementation of schoolwide behavioral support: The High Five program. *Journal of Positive Behavioral Support, 2*(4) [On-line]. Available: www.pbis.org/english/index.html.

15. Colvin, G., & Fernandez, B. (2000). Sustaining effective support systems in an elementary school: Keeping the plan operating for almost a decade. *Journal of Positive Behavioral Support, 2*(4) [On-line]. Available: www.pbis.org/english/index.html.

16. Dwyer & Osher. (2000).

17. *Schoolwide PBIS.* [On-line]. Available: www.pbis.org/English/main.php3?name=Schoolwide_PBIS.

18. Sugai, G. M., Kame'enui, E. J., Horner, R. H., & Simmons, D. C. (1999). *Effective instructional and behavioral support systems: A schoolwide approach to discipline and early literacy* [On-line]. Available: ericec.org/osep/eff-syst.htm.

19. Sugai et al. (1999). Effective instructional and behavioral support systems: A schoolwide approach to discipline and early literacy [On-line]. Available: ericec.org/osep/eff-syst.htm.

20. Brooks et al. (2000); DeJong, W. (1994). *Preventing interpersonal violence among youth: An introduction to school, community and mass media strategies* (Publication No. 1994–387–167:38). Washington, DC: U.S. Government Printing Office; Thornton et al. (2000); Tolan, P., & Guerra, N. (1998). *What works in reducing adolescent violence: An empirical review of the field.* Boulder, CO: Institute of Behavioral Science, Regents of the University of Colorado.

21. Quinn, M. M., Gable, R. A., Rutherford, R. B., Howell, K. W., & Hoffman, C. C. Addressing student problem behavior: Creating positive behavioral intervention plans and supports [On-line]. Available:www.air.org/cecp/fba/problembehavior3/text3.htm; Sugai et al. (1999).

22. Kashani, J. H., Jones, M. R., Bumby, K. M., & Thomas, L. A. (1999). Youth violence: Psychosocial risk factors, treatment, prevention, and recommendations. *Journal of Emotional and Behavioral Disorders, 7,* 200–210; Sugai et al. (2000).

23. Sugai et al. (2000).

24. Forness, S. R. (1998). Early detection and primary prevention in systems of care. In P. Leone & S. M. Meisel (Eds.), *Linking Schools and Communities: Conference Proceedings.* College Park, MD: University of Maryland Center for the Study of Troubling Behavior; Walker, H. M., & Severson, H. H. (1990). *Systematic screening for behavior disorders.* Longmont, CO: Sopris West.

25. Nelson et al. (1999).

26. For a discussion of PACT, see Hammond, W. R., Kadis, P., & Yung, B. (1990). *Positive Adolescents Choices Training (PACT): Preliminary findings of the effects of a school-based violence prevention program for African American adolescents.* Columbus, Ohio: Ohio Commission on Minority Health. (ERIC Document Reproduction Service No. ED 326 812); Thornton et al. (2000); U.S. General Accounting Office (1995). *School safety: Promising initiatives for addressing school violence* (GAO-HEHS-95–106). Report to the Ranking Minority Member, Subcommittee on Children and Families, Committee on Labor and Human Resources, U.S. Senate. Washington, DC: Author; Yung, B. R., & Hammond, W. R. (1993). Evaluation and activity report: *Positive Adolescents Choices Training Program.* Final grant report to the Ohio Governor's Office of Criminal Justice Services, 92-DG-BO1–7138.

27. For a discussion of First Step to Success, see Golly, A. M., Stiller, B., & Walker, H. M. (1998). First step to success: Replication and social validation of an early intervention program. *Journal of Emotional and Behavioral Disorders, 6,* 243–250; Kashani, J. H., Jones, M. R., Bumby, K. M., & Thomas, L. A. (1999). Youth violence: Psychosocial risk factors, treatment, prevention, and recommendations. *Journal of Emotional and Behavioral Disorders, 7,* 200–210; Quinn, M. M., Osher, D., Hoffman, C., & Hanley (1998). *Safe, drug-free, and*

effective schools for ALL students: What works! Washington, DC: Center for Effective Collaboration and Practice, American Institutes for Research; Walker, H. M., Colvin, G., & Ramsey, E. (1995). *Antisocial behavior in school: Strategies and best practices.* Pacific Grove, CA: Brooks/Cole.

28. Lane, K. L., Umbreit, J., & Beebe-Frankenberger, M. E. (1999). Functional assessment research on students with or at risk for EBD: 1990 to the present. *Journal of Positive Behavior Intervention, 1,* 101–111; O'Neill, R. E., Horner, R. H., Albin, R. W., Sprague, J. R., Storey, K., & Newton, J. S. (1997). *Functional assessment and program development for problem behavior: A practical handbook* (2nd ed.). Pacific Grove, CA: Brooks/Cole.

29. For a discussion of the use of functional behavior assessment, see Chandler, L. K., Dahlquist, C. M., Repp, A. C., & Feltz, C. (1999). The effects of team-based functional assessment on the behavior of students in classroom settings. *Exceptional Children, 66,* 101–122; Grandy, S. E., & Peck, S. M. (1997). The use of functional assessment and self-management with a first grader. *Child and Family Behavior Therapy, 19*(2), 29–43; Heckaman, K., Conroy, M., Fox, J., & Chait, A. (2000). Functional assessment-based intervention research on students with or at risk for emotional and behavioral disorders in school settings. *Behavioral Disorders, 25,* 196–210; Sugai, G., Horner, R. H., & Sprague, J. (1999). Functional assessment-based behavior support planning: Research-to-practice-to-research. *Behavioral Disorders, 24,* 223–227; Walker, H. M., & Severson, H. H. (1990). *Systematic screening for behavior disorders.* Longmont, CO: Sopris West.

30. Yell, M. L., & Shriner, J. G. (1997). The IDEA amendments of 1997: Implications for special and general education teachers, administrators, and teacher trainers. *Focus on Exceptional Children, 30,* 1–19.

31. For a discussion of alternative programs see Cox, S. M., Davidson, S. M., & Bynum, T. S. (1995). A meta-analytic assessment of delinquency-related outcomes of alternative education programs. *Crime and Delinquency, 41,* 219–234; Gottfredson, D. C. (2001). *Schools and delinquency.* New York: Cambridge University Press; Quinn, M. M., & Rutherford, R. B. (1998). *Alternative programs for students with social, emotional or behavior problems.* Reston, VA: Council for Exceptional Children.

32. Quinn & Rutherford. (1998). p. 19.

33. Office of Justice Programs. (1999). *The appropriate use of security technologies in U.S. schools.* Washington, DC: U.S. Department of Justice.

34. Nieto, M. (1999). *Security and crime prevention strategies in California public schools.* Sacramento: California State Library, California Research Bureau. (ERIC Document Reproduction Service No. ED 438 704)

35. Brotherton, D. C. (1996). The contradictions of suppression: Notes from a study of approaches to gangs in three public high schools. *Urban Review, 28,* 95–117.

36. Brooks et al. (2000); Mayer, M. J., & Leone, P. E. (1999). A structural analysis of school violence and disruption: Implications for creating safer schools. *Education and Treatment of Children, 22,* 333–358; Mendel, R. A. (2000). *Less hype, more help: Reducing juvenile crime, what works—and what doesn't.* Washington, DC: American Youth Policy Forum. (ERIC Document

Reproduction Service No. ED 445 285). Research and policy analysis suggest that punitive, control-type approaches do little to solve continuing problems of school violence and disruption.

37. U.S. Department of Education. (2000). *Twenty-second annual report to Congress on the implementation of the Individuals with Disabilities Education Act.* Jessup, MD: Education Publications Center.

38. Brier, N. (1995). Predicting antisocial behavior in youngsters displaying poor academic achievement: A review of risk factors. *Journal of Developmental and Behavioral Pediatrics, 16,* 271–276; Rylance, B. J. (1997). Predictors of high school graduation or dropping out for youths with severe emotional disturbances. *Behavioral Disorders, 23,* 5–17; Skiba, R. J., Peterson, R. L., & Williams, T. (1997). Office referrals and suspensions: Disciplinary intervention in middle schools. *Education and Treatment of Children, 20,* 295–315.

39. Quinn, M. M., Kavale, K. A., Mathur, S. R., Rutherford, R. B., & Forness, S. R. (1999). A meta-analysis of social skill interventions for students with emotional or behavioral disorders. *Journal of Emotional and Behavioral Disorders, 7,* 54–64.

JOSEPH C. GAGNON *is a doctoral candidate in the Department of Special Education at the University of Maryland, College Park.*

PETER E. LEONE *is a professor in the Department of Special Education at the University of Maryland, College Park.*

It is possible to create schools that are humane, caring places where discipline issues are minimized.

5

The best approach to safety is to fix schools and support children and staff

David M. Osher, Susan Sandler,
Cameron Lynn Nelson

COMPARED TO OTHER PARTS of society, schools are relatively safe.[1] Yet too many students fear going to school, too many teachers view teaching as dangerous, and too many parents, particularly those from economically disadvantaged communities, worry that their children will neither be able to learn or be safe at school.

Common wisdom says it is necessary to choose between a school's safety and keeping all students in school, particularly in schools serving students of color, economically disadvantaged students, and students with emotional and behavioral disabilities. However, the findings of our research, *Safe, Drug-Free and Effective Schools for All Students: The Role of Education in Systems of Care*, and *Turning to Each Other*, indicate that it is not necessary to choose between a school's safety and keeping all students in school.[2] Our research suggests that creating a school that is committed to keeping and educating all of its students can make the school physically and psychologically safer for all students while increasing their ability to learn and their teachers' ability to teach.

The consistency of our findings should not be surprising. Empirical data suggest that the best approach to safety is to fix schools

NEW DIRECTIONS FOR YOUTH DEVELOPMENT, NO. 92, WINTER 2001 © WILEY PERIODICALS, INC.

and support children. Previous research has found that schools may set the stage for or reinforce inappropriate behavior, reactive and punitive approaches can exacerbate discipline problems, segregating antisocial youth or removing them from school environments reinforces antisocial behavior, mechanical approaches to school removal will include too many false positives and false negatives to be fair or effective, and "expelling or suspending a student for making a threat must not be a substitute for careful threat assessment and a considered, consistent policy of interventions."[3]

Research also suggests strategies for creating supportive school environments. These strategies employ approaches to reduce discipline problems and promote prosocial behavior and academic achievement that are positive, comprehensive, individualized, and culturally competent.[4] Our work suggests that schools can link effective interventions and implement them in a caring, supportive, and culturally competent manner. When schools do this, they can reduce problematic student behavior and reduce staff reliance on punishment and removal as disciplinary tools. In so doing, these schools keep youth in school, where they can develop the social and academic skills necessary for a successful transition to adulthood.[5]

Research summary

The Safe, Drug-Free and Effective Schools for All Students: What Works project was commissioned by the U.S. Department of Education's Safe and Drug Free Schools (SDFS) Programs and the Office of Special Education Programs (OSEP). The schools described by the project were selected through multiple-gated expert nomination to identify schools that effectively prevented disruptive behaviors though schoolwide collaborations that included activities funded by SDFS and OSEP. Two-day site visits were conducted by two researchers and an expert panel of ten stakeholders that included representatives of youth, families, school bus drivers, and teachers; teacher union representatives; principals and superintendents; researchers; state officials from education, mental health, and juvenile justice; and representatives from the U.S.

Department of Education. Each site visit included focus groups with students, families, general and special educators, administrators and school board members, and community agency representatives.

The Role of Education in Systems of Care was part of a series of monographs commissioned by the Center for Mental Health Services to examine promising practices in systems of care.[6] Communities were selected through expert nomination and review of outcome data and two-day site visits conducted by two researchers who met with families, youth, educators, and mental health providers.

The research for the *Turning to Each Other, Not on Each Other* report began with a national expert nomination process to identify model schools that successfully prevent racial bias in discipline by using caring, thoughtful approaches. A final selection yielded eight schools from which qualitative and quantitative information was gathered as interviews and documents. Most of the schools in Osher's two studies and all of the schools in Sandler's study match what some view as the problematic demographic profile: predominantly students of color, with the majority of students qualifying for free or reduced-price lunch. Notably, not one of these schools relied on discipline approaches that exclude, alienate, and discard students to create a compelling learning environment. Instead, the schools we studied created an environment of physical and emotional safety in which there were low or diminishing rates of disciplinary referral and school removal.

A three-level approach to preventing violence

The schools we studied employed a strategic, coordinated, three-level approach that enabled school staff to address the academic, behavioral, and emotional needs of all students. This approach has been conceptualized by Osher and his colleagues in a number of other publications.[7] It is consistent with the Institute of Medicine's reconceptualization of prevention and treatment, the Office of Juvenile Justice and Delinquency Prevention's approach to serious and chronic violent offending, and schoolwide approaches to positive behavioral support.[8] This approach is pictured in Figure 5.1.

The bottom layer of the triangle is the schoolwide foundation, which involves activities directed at all students, staff, and families. This foundation provides a base on which the second level of the triangle, early intervention, rests. Schools committed to the success of all students intervene quickly when they notice that some students, staff, or families are having problems. In some cases, these interventions are insufficiently powerful to address intense, protracted, or complex problems. In these cases, schools that are committed to serving all students employ intensive and individualized interventions (the top of the triangle) to enable their more troubled students to succeed.

We will employ this three-level model to show how schools reduce problematic behavior in a proactive and culturally competent manner.

Figure 5.1. A three-level approach to preventing violence

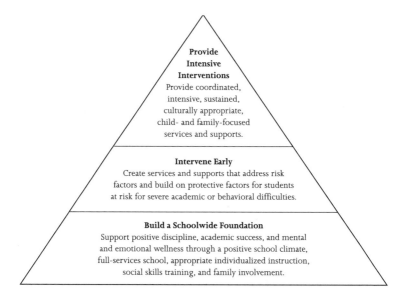

Schoolwide foundation

Safe schools provide all students with the supports and skills they need to feel connected to the school and to be effective learners and problem solvers. In addition, this foundation provides all students and staff with the supports and skills needed to develop and foster appropriate behaviors and healthy emotional adjustment. This foundation, elaborated on elsewhere,[9] involves the following factors:

- Compassionate, caring, respectful staff who model appropriate behaviors, create a climate of emotional support, and are committed to working with all students
- Developmentally appropriate and culturally competent programs for all children that teach and reinforce social and problem-solving skills
- Teachers and staff who are trained to teach and connect with culturally and linguistically diverse learners and to support positive school and classroom behaviors
- Engaging culturally competent and linguistically appropriate curricula and pedagogy
- Staff collaboration and collaboration with families and students
- Culturally proficient leadership[10]
- A school culture and structure that help all students connect with the school, view themselves as learners, succeed as learners, remain in school, support other students, and behave appropriately
- A student-centered school community that respects young people and integrates their culture into the school
- High expectations and high levels of support for all students

We elaborate on two elements of the foundation here: operationalizing a caring culture and operationalizing a relevant culture.

Operationalizing a caring culture. School is frequently an aversive place for many, marked by staff and student hostility.[11] Many of the schools that we observed established a caring culture that infused all aspects of schooling, providing a sense of belonging for students and helping them identify with the school community, and therefore feeding their desire to support the school. A teacher at El Puente Academy for Peace and Justice in Brooklyn, New York, said, "When there is a sense of community, the rules make sense."[12] Adults' respectful, caring demeanor toward students sets an example that students emulate. Because adults in these school cultures are committed to developing the potential of each student, they approach difficulties with a problem-solving, solution-driven orientation. This caring attitude was shared by students.

One of the key factors enabling schools to operationalize a caring culture is a strong shared mission. When school staff have a common orientation and goals that incorporate caring, they work to make sure that every aspect of the school and each new situation reflects this mission. They examine traditional structures and practices of schooling and change what gets in the way of creating a caring environment.

Schools' missions can be as simple as being a community, as in the case of the San Francisco Community School. They can be as complicated as the twelve guiding principles of the El Puente Academy for Peace and Justice, which include elements such as respect, mastery, and creating community. Sometimes the mission is not even formalized. Oakhurst Elementary in Decatur, Georgia, has no written mission, but staff, students, and parents describe a place where students and parents are made to feel welcome and special.

Once the mission is in place, it shapes everything from grading to celebrations to configurations of students and staff. For example, the River East School in East Harlem in New York City expresses its values for enacting a community in which everyone is well known and cared for in many ways. Each classroom encompasses two grade levels, so students stay with the same teacher for two years, a period that allows them to develop a deeper, stronger relationship with their teacher. They are also former classmates of students in other grades, having graduated to the next class before or after them.

In addition to the grade configurations, River East builds community through gatherings. The entire school comes together weekly for a town meeting, run by the different classes on a rotating basis. This gathering is just one type of meeting. Each classroom has a meeting area, used for class meetings three or four times a day, when students review the day's schedule as a group, work out the challenges of daily life together, and practice solving problems as a community.

The River East staff also express their mission through their grading policy. Each student receives multipage narrative reports instead of grades. Although this grading policy requires an enormous amount of time, staff believe it is worthwhile as an expression of their value of knowing each child well as a unique individual and engaging in meaningful dialogue with parents.

These schools demand a great deal from staff and have structures in place that support the staff's capacity to sustain a caring environment. This capacity is supported by intensive training and support on positive behavioral approaches, effective pedagogy, support for staff collaboration (such as planning and meeting time), and a problem-solving culture that focuses on continuous improvement. Training and support are ongoing so that staff master new approaches to schooling. Collaboration reduces the isolation of individual teachers and staff members and helps build a schoolwide team. The problem-solving approach enables staff members to discuss problems openly and seek solutions rather than blaming students, family, or staff for problems. Florida's Jesse Keane Elementary School in Lakeland, Florida, and Cleveland Elementary School in Tampa, Florida, engage the whole school in strategic planning efforts to meet students' needs better. A Jesse Keane parent expressed the impact of this approach by observing that parents never hear teachers say, "I'm having a problem." Rather, they are approached by school staff with phrases such as, "We need to work on . . . " or "I have an idea for you."

A teacher at Jesse Keane suggested the links between teacher support and teacher caring:

Teachers everywhere need to stick with something long enough to see the results. It's never easy to start anything, and with so many new programs coming down, you try something for awhile, and if you don't see fast, amazing results, then you throw it out. This program is excellent, but it takes a real determination; it takes everybody wanting the same thing for their kids at school. If they just stick with it and are consistent with it, it makes all the difference in the world. It will help their kids no matter what area they're coming from, whether it's a low socioeconomic area; it doesn't matter where they come from. The kids understand that the teachers care about them and want them to succeed.

Operationalizing a relevant culture. There is often a strong disconnect between many students of color and their schools, reflected in low attendance rates, limited academic participation, and unsafe and hostile school environments. Culturally and linguistically diverse students often feel a disconnect between the school and their home culture.[13] Moreover, the self-concept of many children of color may be "lessened in school settings."[14] Some schools address these challenges by building a school culture grounded in students' cultures, knowledge, and interests. These schools use their cultural relevance to deepen their students' identification with the school, their positive self-concept, and their engagement in learning. In turn, this identification and engagement helps students to be positive, contributing members of the school community, upholding its norms and expectations.

El Puente Academy for Peace and Justice designs its curriculum to be relevant to students on many levels: culture and heritage, youth culture, the issues in their communities, and self-expression through the arts. El Puente's use of themes illustrates the school's curriculum approach. In addition to the grade-level, subject-area curriculum, every year the school has a theme that all study through many disciplines and that serves as the basis for artistic work and projects that benefit the community. Sugar was picked as one yearly theme because of its relevance to the El Puente community. Many of the families of El Puente students and staff come from Puerto Rico and the Dominican Republic, where sugar is a major export crop. The role of sugar in these countries' economies has had a major impact on the families of El Puente. At the same time, their neighborhood is home to a sugar refinery, which influences the neighborhood's economy and pollutes the environment.

School staff require training that helps change habits of mind so that they do not view differences as deficits and so that their teaching approaches can be informed by students' worldview.[15] This training can help them understand and counter the dynamics of racial and cultural power and privilege.[16] Some of the schools we studied drew on an understanding of the dynamics of racism to inform how they work with students and families, examine their own possible racial biases, and encourage other members of the school community to feel comfortable about bringing up issues of racism. For example, the San Francisco Community School is devoting considerable professional development resources to helping all staff learn to deinstitutionalize racism.

Intervening early: A relational approach

Early intervention is necessary for students who are at risk of academic failure or behavior problems (as well as for staff who are experiencing problems and families who are not able to connect with the school). Early interventions can be selective (for example, for populations of children who are placed at risk, such as children who have experienced abuse) or indicated (for example, for individual children whose behavior indicates that they are at risk). We have described these indicators elsewhere.[17] To be effective, however, school staff must be sensitive to student needs, and their interventions must be done in a culturally competent manner that does not stigmatize students, alienate their parents, or create self-fulfilling prophecies or dynamics.

These schools attend to warning signs as indicators of the need for additional support. Wherever possible, they provide this support without labels and without removing the students from regular classes. Westerly, Rhode Island, uses collaborative teams of special and regular educators to help students with diverse learning and behavioral needs to succeed in mainstream environments. Between 1990 and 1995, Westerly's schools moved from an initial two to fifty-six teams while at the same time reducing self-contained classrooms that segregated students with emotional and behavioral disorders from thirteen to two. The Englewood, New Jersey, school system provides another example of providing support without labeling. In order to promote cultural competence and decrease the incidence of stigma and victim blaming, they host weekend getaways for teachers, primary caretakers, and students. These retreats are designed to begin a process of moving away from blaming others for children's behavior. Participants are expected to move toward self-accountability. These retreats provide opportunities to value and respect the practices of other cultures by understanding that "different" does not mean "wrong" in cross-cultural interactions.

The schools that we studied had developed the capacity to identify problems early and respond to them in a sensitive, strengths-based, and individualized manner. We call this approach relational because its efficacy relies on strong relationships between staff and students and families. Adults in the school pay sufficient attention to each student to notice when something may be wrong. Once they notice, they arrange to spend time with that student and his or her family. That time may be spent in many ways: learning about what is going on with the student, problem solving, teaching skills, or just talking. School adults draw on a preexisting positive relationship to understand the student's current situation and be positioned as a confidant or respected adviser in the student's and parent's eyes.

Tampa's Cleveland Elementary School, 97 percent of whose students are eligible for free or reduced-fee lunch, provides an example of a relational response. Cleveland's principal stands outside the school each morning to greet parents as they drop off their children and welcome each student by name as they enter the school. When she notices that a student looks troubled, she or another staff member who knows the child talks to the student, looks into any problems, and then discusses what they have learned with the parents. School staff walk many of the children home to the nearby housing project, where they talk to the parents as they drop off the students. At Oakhurst Elementary School, staff work hard to build relationships with families that they can draw on to detect problems as soon as possible and work them out. Teachers give parents weekly progress reports so they are aware of both their children's progress and the efforts the teacher is making with their child. Frequent communication not only allows staff and parents to pick up problems early on, but prevents the distrust that can arise if the first time a parent learns of an academic problem is from the report card. School staff give parents their home numbers so as to be more accessible.

This relational perspective enables schools to handle discipline problems in an effective and positive manner. Instead of suspending a student, the principal at Oakhurst Elementary will often drive the child in question home and sit down and talk with the parent. Often, staff and families develop and then collaborate on solutions that reward the student for incremental improvements. At the Lane School in Eugene, Oregon, a problem is viewed as a teachable moment, that is, an opportunity to teach or review skills. Westerly's schools employ creative alternatives to suspension that build on the strengths of students; for example, an older student might tutor a younger student.

Understanding the causes of student misbehavior and developing strategies to address them is key to early intervention. At New York's Central Park East Secondary School, adults who feel students are not meeting expectations begin by gathering information. They might talk to colleagues who know the student. Then a meeting is held, with just the student or including the student's adviser, family, or others, focusing on identifying goals, problem solving, and possibly determining consequences for the student. Follow-up is an important part of this process in an effort to acknowledge the student for improvements or develop further plans.

Functional assessment, a technique that enables teachers and staff to understand the context of behavioral problems, can be employed in a relational manner so as to involve students and families in the analysis of student behavior.[18] Some schools employ these tools only for children with disabilities and only after a disciplinary problem arises; schools in Narragansett, Rhode Island, employ a more proactive approach. Narragansett schools employ functional assessment when any child (not just those with identified disabilities) is first referred for services. Functional assessment in Narragansett is not an afterthought that is included only when there is a major disciplinary issue, as outlined in special education regulations.

Relational approaches make sense to students. Four students from a Lane County, Oregon, middle school expressed the importance of such an approach with the following acronym:

T   Talk to students; don't just punish them.
L   Make it clear you're there where the kids are. Let them know you're there.
S   Teachers should care more, don't put down students, be nicer.
A   Talk to students instead of suspending them. Suspension doesn't solve a problem; it's just provoking.

Intensive interventions emphasizing student growth, learning, and responsibility

Some students require more intensive interventions. Elsewhere, we have recommended that schools make available to their students an intensive array of individualized interventions such as special education services and supports, strengths-based individualized wrap-around planning and supports, school-based mental health services, and multisystemic therapies.[19]

Schools in East Baltimore, Maryland, provide individualized school-based mental health services in a culturally competent manner. East Baltimore Mental Health Partnership's School-Based Program maintains at least one clinician in each of its nineteen schools who primarily works with individual children referred by their teachers or the principal. Clinicians work with referred students and their families to discover the source of a student's emotional or behavioral problem and identify strengths that can be leveraged to address those identified needs.

Intensive interventions work best when they build on schoolwide efforts as well as early interventions. For example, a number of East

Baltimore schools have incorporated schoolwide curricular programs into their plans to prevent or intervene early with violent and aggressive behaviors. East Baltimore's clinicians are part of the teams that staff the after-school programs, so that they may observe and address any problems that may arise with the students. They also help staff a summer camp for children and youth with serious emotional disturbance who might otherwise be excluded from field trips or extracurricular activities because of their behavior. The partnership provides teachers with training to help them identify and assist students who are at risk of or who exhibit early signs of aggressive behaviors, attempting to prevent these children from getting into greater trouble.

Even with intensive and comprehensive supports in place, however, some students still act out and commit disciplinary infractions. How do these schools maintain the sense of safety in the face of such an eventuality? Many of the schools employ interventions that help the students learn from their actions, take responsibility, make amends, and change their behavior. At the same time, because these interventions downplay exclusionary and judgmental approaches, the student stays identified with the school community and continues to buy in to its norms and expectations. Finally, these interventions embody the school's caring ethic and continue to model a compassionate code of behavior in the school community.

The East Baltimore School-Based Program seeks to create a community within the classroom that fosters positive relationships among the students. A student exhibiting problem behaviors can be removed from the classroom temporarily so that the school personnel and the clinician can work closely with him or her to identify the function (or reason) behind the inappropriate behavior. During the time out of the classroom, school personnel and the clinicians help the student develop appropriate skills for expressing his or her needs. The process of reintegrating the student into the class includes the student's apologizing to the class and the teacher for the inappropriate behavior. The student also identifies a way to make up for the disruption if that is warranted and asks the teacher and peers to help him or her practice positive behaviors. The student returns to the class with a plan he or she jointly developed with teacher and peers.

The strength of this community-within-classrooms model is that a sense of community and relatedness is actively encouraged among the students. Disruptive behavior is viewed as an event that affects the entire classroom community, and all have an interest in addressing it. In addition, students are held accountable for their inappropriate behaviors and helped to develop positive individual and community behaviors.

At El Puente, when something serious happens that violates the sense of safety of the community, the school's crisis team, composed of staff from El Puente, goes into action. After gathering the facts and requesting feedback and input from staff, the team develops a plan and informs the staff. It is important that the adults who work with the student feel that their opinion is heard and to be invested in the solution.

The crisis team's plan might include the principal's meeting with each class, giving the teacher and students the opportunity to discuss how they were affected by the behavior. Students feel safe at the school and are concerned when that sense of safety has been undermined. Meanwhile, the student involved in the incident might be temporarily taken out of class and sent to work in one of the staff offices. Sometimes a student might be suspended in order to have time to reflect and is given specific questions to think about. Staff help the student take responsibility for what happened. As the situation gets resolved, there is a process to bring the student back into the community. This can include the student's meeting with the people he or she has hurt or a meeting with representatives of the El Puente community (students and adults) in which the student formally reenters the community.

In some cases, it may be necessary to change the setting in which the child attends school. Oregon's Lane School is an alternative school that exemplifies a positive environment that prepares students and the mainstream schools for the return of the students. Lane is small, enabling students to receive the structure, attention, and skills they need to improve their behavior and their academic performance and prepare to return to their neighborhood schools. Interventions are highly individualized, and the emphasis is on effective problem solving through communication with others and on improving each student's academic performance. The supervisor of Lane School emphasizes the need for efficient and effective structures that lead to the creation of "civil classroom and school climates." This includes having a system of clear rules, teaching students alternative responses to anger, and then reinforcing those skills, intervening in aggression early, deterring violent behaviors with clear consequences, and emphasizing academics consistently.

The school is organized in a level system through which students advance as they meet their individualized behavioral and academic goals, which they help set for themselves. In addition, Lane School uses a system of rewards for positive behavior and involves parents and community agencies to a high degree to help ensure that the needs of each student have been met. Lane School fosters students' academic and social success by creating a caring, respectful environment that provides them with positive feedback and experiences. As students are prepared to return to their home schools, a Lane School consultant visits the school to assist in preparations for the return of the student. The consultants work with student advocates or other school personnel to discuss positive behavioral support methods and other interventions to use with students who exhibit behavioral problems. During these visits, consultants also work with students at those schools who have been referred for chronic behavioral problems.

Structures and resource deployment

In order to build and maintain the types of programs described, certain structures and types of resources must be in place. Comprehensive and meticulous approaches to schooling occur only when conditions are set to support them. Factors such as the way staff deployment and the use of their time, school size, and the quality of leadership all determine the potential for creating a truly safe school.

The schools that we studied deployed staff so that staff could help build a caring community that develops and sustains relationships with students and their families. At River East Elementary School, staff assigned by the district to do clerical work or security are brought into the classroom, so that there will be more adults working with the students. Cleveland Elementary School employs its Title I resources to hire a full-time social worker to link with families and full-time school psychologists to support teacher problem solving and help the school implement a social skills curriculum. Westerly's schools already had such staff, but coordinated their efforts so as to help create an environment that addressed the individual needs of all students.

Teachers are frequently burdened by time pressures.[20] Not surprisingly, time is another important resource that is carefully apportioned in these schools. Staff members of the schools we studied go to great and often creative lengths to create time to meet together for professional development and planning. At Pharr-San Juan-Alamo High School in San Juan, Texas, staff development activities are offered four times over the course of the day so that all staff may participate during their preparation periods.

Training works when staff do not experience it as a burden. Hence, resources are very important to support staff planning and development. For example, District 4J in Lane, Oregon, appropriated money to enable school staff to get together and "build their compassion." In many schools, staff put in far more than the meeting time required of them in their union contracts, these demands can be built into union contracts. Westerly's National Education Association unit successfully negotiated a contract that compensates teachers for training.

School size is a key factor. Many of the schools in the studies were small, and the staff at these schools stressed how vital that size is to their ability to create a caring community. Smallness makes it possible for students and staff to know each other well, create a sense of community, and gather as a school for regular meetings. Visitors to the small schools noticed that student tour guides seemed to know the teacher of each class and what was going on in the class. Staff were better able to work out problems with students who were not in their class because they knew each other.

This intimate, homelike feeling can be replicated at the larger schools, but there are more obstacles to overcome. Large schools must develop ways for students to feel known and have a sense of belonging. For example, DeWitt Clinton High School in the Bronx really seems like home to its forty-three hundred students, according to their comments about the school. The school cultivates a warm tone through celebrations, slogans, abundant supportive services, and a myriad of activities for students, as well as a strong, caring ethic among the staff. But the school also actively finds ways to bring in experiences of smallness. DeWitt Clinton is divided into twelve houses, each with a supervisor, guidance counselor, and family outreach assistant. If a student misses a few days at school, one of the house staff calls or goes to the student's house—not to intrude but to show the school cares. The students know that they are not lost in the crowd and that school staff are following them closely, determined to ensure their success.

Finally, culturally proficient leadership plays a significant role. This was most apparent in poorly performing schools that had shown significant improvement. When asked what brought about the change, leaders, especially principals, were cited. These leaders "reculture" the schools. A competent leader was described as a person or group that embodied the value of problem solving and serving all students, sharing information, and helping develop and sustain a sense of ownership and pride among staff, students, and parents. Effective leadership helped model a commitment to collaboration, serving all students, working respectfully with all families, and maintaining a commitment to continuous improvement. Effective leadership, a Westerly school psychologist stated, was necessary to enable staff to "stay focused, take chances, and stay extremely determined to work toward that end."

A trained staff with strong leadership can make a difference. An itinerant school psychologist compared the Jesse Keane

Elementary School in Lakeland, Florida, with other schools that she works in where the expectations are often that her role is to test and remove children with behavior problems:

> In terms of my role as a school psychologist, this school has been great. This is the best school that I have. I love this school. When I come in and we're working with a kid or talking about a child, I can feel comfortable to throw out ideas for intervention, and the teachers are receptive. They also come in with a problem-solving model, and they're not looking for a quick fix. They're looking for ways to help this child learn better and learn appropriate skills for the classroom. We can have a dialogue about interventions that might work, and what they're willing to do and feel comfortable doing, and if they need help, I can then come in. The whole mentality from the administration down is that we want to work with all the kids and want them all to be successful, and so we're going to do what we need to do to accomplish that. Here, I'm part of a team. I know that my testing may come down the road, but it would be in the best interest of the child.

Turning schools around for all students

School change is never easy but always possible. Both techniques and models for these transformations are available.[21]

Transforming schools and institutionalizing change require strategic long-term efforts that addresses what Boykin referred to as the outer and inner structure of school reform—the interventions themselves, as well as how they are experienced by stakeholders.[22] Still, it is possible to build a schoolwide foundation that operationalizes a caring culture. It is also possible to develop a capacity to respond relationally to early warning signs and provide intensive interventions. These efforts empower students, staff, and families by changing relationships between them, as well as by providing accessible training and support so that students can meet high behavioral and academic standards.

These efforts can pay off for all students, not just those who are at risk. Westerly teachers received intensive training that was not just "piled on top of existing classroom duties."[23] Families experienced welcoming schools where their active participation was facilitated by relational approaches that respected their expertise and responded to their individual needs.[24] And all children benefited through the strengthened ability of teachers to respond to the individual needs of all students and through planning centers to which students could self-refer for emotional, behavioral, and academic support, as well as with links to social services. The payoff was improved schoolwide behavior and academic performance. A Westerly elementary school teacher who was selected by her site-based management team to serve as the school leader described the change in her school:

> I've taught in Westerly twenty-five years, and things have changed drastically over that period of time. We have a lot more social issues to deal with. Special education, the school committee, and the administration have been very supportive [when] there's a need. We made a plea a few years back [regarding students] with serious behavioral issues who were literally not able to learn and were impairing the learning of the children who were there ready to learn. With support from everyone concerned, we established the STAR program for these kids on the elementary level. That program has had very good results. We have a consultant who comes, a full-time social worker, and students are able to go to a planning center available on need. We meet regularly to improve the program and have received a lot of support.

Recommendations

Zero tolerance attempts to address school safety through exclusion of those who engage in a certain type or level of behavior. In contrast, the approaches we list here address school safety by preventing problem behavior from occurring or escalating. Much safer than zero-tolerance policies are policies that monitor safety in schools, intervene quickly when schools become unsafe, and provide the supports required to make such intervention unnecessary.

Intervention in schools once they become unsafe may become unnecessary if schools operate in a context of policies that promote strong schoolwide foundations, the development of effective early interventions, and the availability of intensive interventions that emphasize student growth, learning, and accountability. The following recommendations identify what is necessary for this change. At each level, there are needs for professional development, staff time, and financial resources.

Recommendations for putting in place a strong schoolwide foundation

Policymakers can take several steps to make sure that all schools have in place a strong schoolwide foundation that supports and connects all students:

School mission

- Support schools in developing strong, commonly held missions that foster a caring and relevant culture.
- Provide tools that schools can use to develop and deepen a thoughtful shared mission.
- Provide incentives for schools to develop such a mission.
- Allow schools with strong missions to earn flexibility. Schools that demonstrate good outcomes for all students will be given more freedom—for example, in deployment of staff, curriculum and materials, and testing policy.

School size

- Support small schools and schools within schools.
- Provide tools and incentives for large schools to go through a process to break down into smaller schools.
- Support the development of facilities (in shared and freestanding buildings) for small schools.

Professional development and support

- Provide professional development opportunities that expose staff to schools with strong missions and practices that embody caring and relevant cultures.
- Train the staff in problem-solving approaches they can teach students, so that the whole school community has a common lan-

guage for solving problems and is prepared to work together when unexpected challenges arise.

- Provide professional development and support to help staff know their students' cultures and communities and guide them through developing a culture relevant to their students.
- Provide professional development and support on positive approaches to supporting student behavior, as well as on ways of deescalating conflicts.
- Provide professional development and support on effective teaching strategies for students with diverse learning needs.

Time

- Free up time for staff to reflect on their mission and to collaborate and plan ways to incorporate that mission into all relevant aspects of schooling, such as curriculum, testing and grading, events, parent relations, problem solving, and discipline.
- Provide staff time for staff development activities.

Financial resources

- Support professional development and staff release time with financial resources.
- Support small schools with funding for facilities, planning, and potential additional overhead due to smaller scale.

Recommendations for relational early interventions

All of the recommendations supporting a strong schoolwide foundation are equally important for effective early interventions. A schoolwide foundation supports a caring community that allows staff to know the students well. This in turn allows them to notice the first signs of a problem, and the trust of the student and family increases the effectiveness of the intervention. However, additional elements are necessary to bring about a truly effective early intervention system.

- Train staff to identify early warning signs and respond to them appropriately, and provide consultation when necessary.

- Have in place a student support team to help staff respond to early warning signs.

Time

- Provide time for staff to learn about what is going on with students and for problem solving with students and parents. This time might be used in home visits, meetings with the student or the whole family, or frequent written or telephone communication between school staff and the families.

Financial resources

- Support professional development and staff time with financial resources.
- Support small schools with funding for facilities, planning, and potential overhead due to smaller scale.

Recommendations for intensive interventions

Having a schoolwide foundation and intervening early greatly increase the success of intensive interventions that emphasize student growth, learning, and responsibility. Because of the strong schoolwide foundation, intensive interventions are not undermined by an impersonal, alienating, or chaotic school environment. School staff can use their deep understanding of their mission to select social service providers who employ approaches that are consistent with and enhance the school culture. The following additional features must be in place to have successful intensive interventions:

Professional development and support

- Provide professional development on when to refer a student to a professional and how to collaborate effectively with social service professionals.
- Provide tools, guidelines, and resource directories that schools can use to select appropriate social service providers who can collaborate with schools and families to meet the needs of their

students in a culturally appropriate way and enhance the school culture.

Time
- Free up staff time to meet and collaborate with social service providers who are working with their students.

Financial resources
- Support professional development and staff time with financial resources.
- Provide resources for schools to pay for intensive interventions for the students who need it.

Conclusion

We are at risk of losing another generation of young people who, in spite of their strengths, are placed at risk by poverty, racism, access to guns, violence in the media and their communities, and schools that are not always organized to meet their needs. Schools can be "lifelines . . . opportunities which potentially lead from pathways associated with deviant or destructive outcomes."[25] For schools to play this role, they need to protect and hold on to all their students and help them develop the academic, social, and emotional competencies they will need to succeed as adults.

The schools we studied explode the myth that it is necessary to choose between harsh discipline of students and safe, academically productive schools. Their staff demonstrate that it is possible to create schools for all students that are humane, caring places where discipline issues are minimal and when they do arise are viewed as opportunities that can contribute to growth and development. Equally important, these schools demonstrate that it is possible to turn around schools with significant discipline problems. The principal of one such school, the Jesse Keane Elementary School, described the impact:

I've been in this school for twenty years, and this is the best thing I've ever seen for helping children manage their behavior. I used to have children lined up all day long for discipline. The big difference is that now teachers are able to teach. I'm able to get in the classrooms more; we're able to do what we're supposed to be doing as educators. The neatest thing of all is that the children now have skills, and teachers have skills. The children are able to internalize. Before, the teachers and administrators were preaching when a child made a bad choice; now, the child immediately takes responsibility for his or her own behavior.

Our findings do not stand alone. Comprehensive models have been developed in both regular education and special education to address the needs of students placed at risk, and many authors have demonstrated how teachers can teach in a relational and culturally responsive manner.[26] It is important that these lines of work come together so that schools can effectively teach and hold on to all students. Regular education initiatives can benefit from effective special education techniques that address individual needs, and special education approaches can benefit from effective schoolwide approaches that address race, language, and culture. The powerful combination of these approaches can help educators create excellent schools where parents want to send their children, where children want to attend, and where teachers want to teach.

Notes

1. U.S. Departments of Education and Justice. (2000). *Annual report on school safety.* Washington, DC: Authors.

2. Quinn, M .M., Osher, D., Hoffman, C. C., & Hanley, T. V. (1998). *Safe, drug-free, and effective schools for all students: The role of education in systems of care.* Washington, DC: U.S. Department of Education; Sandler, S. (2000). *Turning to each other, not on each other: How school communities prevent racial bias in school discipline.* San Francisco: Justice Matters Institute,

3. Federal Bureau of Investigation (2000). *The school shooter: A threat assessment perspective* (p. 32). Washington, DC: FBI. See also Gunter, P. L. & Denny, R. K. (1998). Trends and issues in research regarding academic instruction of students with emotional and behavioral disorders. *Behavioral Disorders, 24*(1), 44–50; Walker, H. M., Colvin, G., & Ramsey, E. (1995). *Antisocial behavior in school: Strategies and best practices.* Pacific Grove, CA: Brooks/Cole; Catalano, R. F., Loeber, R., & McKinney, K. C. (1999, October). *School and community interventions to prevent serious and violent offending.*

Washington, DC: U.S. Department of Justice; Dishion, T., Spracklen, E., Andrews, D., & Patterson, G. (1996). Deviancy training in male adolescent friendships. *Behavior Therapy*, 27, 370–390.

4. Quinn et al. (1998); Balfanz, R., & MacIver, D. (2000). Transforming high-poverty urban middle schools into strong learning institutions: Lessons from the first five years of the Talent Development Middle School. *Journal of Education for Students Placed at Risk*, 5(1) 137–158; Comer, J. (1988). Educating poor and minority children. *Scientific American*, 259(5), 42–48; Jordan, W., McPartland, J., Legters, N., & Balfanz, R. (2000). Creating a comprehensive school reform model: The Talent Development High School with career academies. *Journal of Education for Students Placed at Risk* 5(1–2), 159–183; Dwyer, K., & Osher, D. (2000). *Safeguarding our children: An action guide.* Washington, DC: U.S. Departments of Education and Justice, American Institutes for Research; Sprague, J. R., Sugai, G., Horner, R., & Walker, H. M. (1999). Using office discipline referral data to evaluate school-wide discipline and violence prevention interventions. *OSSC Bulletin*, 42(2) [http://brt. uoregon.edu/ebs/databased.htm]; Noguera, P. (1997). Race, class, and the politics of discipline. *Motion Magazine.* Available: www.inmotionmagazine.com/ pedro35.html; Cartledge, G., Tillman, L.C., & Johnson, C. T. (2001). Professional ethics within the context of student discipline and diversity. *Teacher Education and Special Education*, 24(1), 25–37.

5. Osher, D., Sims, A. & Woodruff, D. (in press). Exploring relationships between inappropriate and ineffective special education services for children of color and their overrepresentation in the juvenile and adult justice systems. In D. Losen (Ed.), *Minority issues in special education.* Cambridge, MA: Civil Rights Project, Harvard University.

6. Woodruff, D., Osher, D., Hoffman, C. C., Gruner, A., King, M. A., Snow, S., & McIntire, J. C. (1998). *The role of education in a system of care: Effectively serving children with emotional or behavioral disorders.* Washington, DC: Center for Effective Collaboration and Practice.

7. Dwyer & Osher. (2000).

8. Institute of Medicine. (1994). *Reducing risks for mental disorders: Frontiers for preventive intervention research.* Washington, DC: National Academy Press.

9. Dwyer & Osher (2000).

10. Lindsey, R. B., Robins, K. N., & Terrell, R. D. (1999). *Cultural proficiency: A manual for school leaders.* Thousand Oaks, CA: Corwin Press; Williams, B. T. (2001). Ethical leadership in schools servicing African American children and youth. *Teacher Education and Special Education*, 24(1), 38–47.

11. Larson, K. (1995). *Redefining troublemakers: Creating an ethic of care and inclusion improve outcomes for adolescents with disabilities and other highest risk adolescents.* Paper presented at the Plenary Presentation Leadership Conference, Washington, D.C., April 1995.

12. The quotation is from an interview for the *Turning to Each Other* research.

13. Jimenez, R. T. (2000). Literacy and the identify development of Latina/o students. *American Educational Research Journal*, 37(4), 971–1000.

14. Campbell-Whatley, G. D., & Comer, J. (2000). Self-concept and African-American student achievement: Related issues of ethics, power and privilege. *Teacher Education and Special Education, 23*(1), 19–31.

15. Cartledge, G., Tillman, L. C., & Johnson, C. T. (2001). Professional ethics within the context of student discipline and diversity. *Teacher Education and Special Education, 24*(1), 25–37; Williams. (2001).

16. Day-Vines, N. L. (2000). Ethics, powers, and privilege: Salient issues in the development of multicultural competencies for teachers serving African American children with disabilities. *Teacher Education and Special Education, 23*(1), 3–18; Gay, G. (2000). *Culturally responsive teaching: Theory, research and practice.* New York: Teachers College Press.

17. Dwyer, K., Osher, D., & Warger, C. (1998). *Early warning, timely response: A guide to safe schools.* Washington, DC: U.S. Department of Education.

18. Quinn, M. M., Gable, R. A., Rutherford, R. B., Nelson, C. M., & Howell, K. W. (1998). *An IEP team's introduction to functional behavioral assessment and behavior intervention plans.* Washington, DC: Center for Effective Collaboration and Practice.

19. Dwyer & Osher. (2000).

20. Huberman, M. (1983). Recipes for busy kitchens: A situational analysis of routine knowledge use in schools. *Knowledge: Creation, Diffusion, Utilization, 4*, 478–510.

21. Adelman, H., & Taylor, L. (1997). *Addressing barriers to student learning: Closing gaps in school/community policy and practice.* Los Angeles: University of California, School Mental Health Project, Department of Psychology; Boykin, A. W. (1986). The triple quandary and the schooling of Afro-American children. In U. Neiser (Ed.), *The school achievement of minority children* (pp. 57–92). Hillsdale, NJ: Erlbaum; Comer. (1988); Edmonds, R. (1986). Characteristics of effective schools. In U. Neisser (Ed.), *The school achievement of minority children* (pp. 93–104). Hillsdale, NJ: Erlbaum; Metz, M. H. (1997). *Keeping students in, gangs out, scores up, alienation down, and the copy machine in working order: Pressures that make urban schools in poverty different.* Paper presented at the Annual Meeting of the American Educational Research Association, Chicago; Murphy, J., Beck, L. G., Crawford, M., Hodges, A., & McGaughy, C. L. (2000). *The productive high school: Empirical evidence.* Albany: State University of New York Press; Osher, D., & Hanley T. V. (1995). Implications of the national agenda to improve results for children and youth with or at risk of serious emotional disturbance. *Special Services in the Schools, 10*(2), 7–36; Schaps, E., Solomon, D., Watson, M., Battistich, V., Schaps, E., & Delucchi, K. (1996). Creating classrooms the students experience as communities. *American Journal of Community Psychology, 24*(6), 719–748; Walker, H. M., et al. (1995).

22. Boykin, A. W. (2000). *Journal of Education for Students Placed at Risk, 5*(1 and 2) [Special issue].

23. Boykin (2000). p. 16.

24. Osher, D., & Keenan, S. (2001). From polarization to partnership: Learning to listen to families. *Reading Today's Youth, 5*, 9–15.

25. Cairns, R. B., & Cairns, B. D. (1994). *Lifelines and risks: Pathways of youth in our time.* Cambridge: Cambridge University Press.

26. Gay. (2000); Ladson-Billings, G. (1994). *The dreamkeepers: Successful teachers of African American children.* San Francisco: Jossey-Bass; Quinn, M. M., Osher, D., Warger, C. L., Hanley, T. V., Bader, B. D., & Hoffman, C. C. (2000). *Teaching and working with children who have emotional and behavioral challenges.* Longmont, CO: Sopris West; Dwyer & Osher (2000).

DAVID M. OSHER *is director of the Center for Effective Collaboration and Practice, American Institutes for Research, Washington, D.C.*

SUSAN SANDLER *is director of the Educational Justice Program at the Justice Matters Institute, San Francisco.*

CAMERON LYNN NELSON *is a research assistant at the Center for Effective Collaboration and Practice, American Institutes for Research, Washington, D.C.*

Prevention of violence in schools must be accompanied by intervention across multiple contexts and the use of consistent but fair consequences that are implemented with children's positive development in mind.

6

Beyond the rhetoric of zero tolerance: Long-term solutions for at-risk youth

Gil G. Noam, Laura A. Warner,
Leigh Van Dyken

AFTER HIGHLY PUBLICIZED acts of school violence, zero tolerance is gaining ground in many communities. Zero tolerance is defined by the American Bar Association as a specific response to student misbehavior where a school automatically and severely punishes students for a variety of infractions, often resulting in expulsion or suspensions and criminal charges.[1] The movement's philosophy is that these consequences and punishments for prohibited behaviors can help protect the entire school community from weapons, drugs, and fighting. If transgressions occur, this approach advocates consistent and inflexible disciplinary consequences (usually suspension or expulsion) in order to avoid uneven treatment of children and to force adults to act decisively. This approach has been used to address not only school violence but also truancy, substance use, and other activities prohibited on school grounds.

NEW DIRECTIONS FOR YOUTH DEVELOPMENT, NO. 92, WINTER 2001 © WILEY PERIODICALS, INC.

Recent research has suggested that the zero-tolerance approach to behavior management may not be effective and may actually be developmentally detrimental to school-age children.[2] A report by the Civil Rights Project at Harvard University notes that "efforts to address guns, drugs and other truly dangerous school situations have spun totally out of control, sweeping up millions of schoolchildren who pose no threat to safety into a net of exclusion from educational opportunities and into criminal prosecution."[3] Proponents of the zero-tolerance approach have done little to demonstrate any short-term or long-term positive effects on children, teachers, or school communities. Skiba and Peterson cite a study conducted by the National Center for Education Statistics that found that after four years, schools with zero-tolerance policies actually experience more unsafe acts and violence than do schools with more flexible discipline policies.[4] Any decrease in violence at schools with zero-tolerance policies is more likely due to the overall national decrease in school violence rather than the zero-tolerance policies themselves. Although media coverage gives the opposite impression, research indicates that school violence has actually decreased over the past ten years, with homicides and shootings being very rare incidents.[5]

Many schools fail to align themselves fully with the developmental needs of adolescents, and zero-tolerance policies are a prime example of this disjunction. In order to develop as citizens, school-age children must learn how to work through conflicts and be given multiple opportunities to correct poor behavior. Strong and trusting relationships with adults that are not based solely on authoritarian models and social control are vital to these processes.

Zero-tolerance policies ("One strike and they're out") deny youth this opportunity to learn from their mistakes. Because of the severity of consequences inherent in these policies, youth are likely to come to see themselves as "bad" or incompetent. As Eccles explains, early adolescents "learn to expect that they will succeed or fail at different tasks."[6] Thus, severely punished students are likely to come to view themselves as deviant, a mind-set that will serve only to propel them into further self-destructive or other-destructive acts. In a more developmentally appropriate system, students would be helped to recognize why their actions were poor choices and that they are capable of better. Actions would not be consequence free, but consequences would be imposed in a way that lets students know that the adults in their life do care about them and are passing negative judgment on the child's actions rather than on the child. Without a clear reordering of priorities, the zero-tolerance movement will not reach its goals; instead, it will only increase the alienation of youth from the adult world and detrimentally segregate many at-risk youth from their peers.

We believe zero-tolerance advocates are misguided in thinking that zero tolerance is a violence-prevention policy. According to their theory, severe punishments will prevent future prohibited acts because punished youth will want to avoid future punishments and their peers will want to avoid the kinds of consequences they have seen inflicted on their classmates. As we mentioned earlier, the data contradict this idea that harsh consequences prevent transgressions. In fact, the blind enforcement of consequences without regard to individual circumstances may make students even less likely to adhere to school rules as they come to see their fate as not in their control and simultaneously lose faith in the fairness of adults and the school policies adults have imposed. As just one example of such faith-undermining incidents, consider the high school senior (incidentally also a National Merit Scholar) who was suspended for five days and not allowed to attend graduation because a steak knife was found in her car.[7] It is believed that the knife fell out of boxes while she was helping her parents move; nevertheless, she was charged with a felony for possession of a weapon on school property.

Zero tolerance also disregards the multifront preventative interventions that may be necessary in dealing with the many risk factors that today's youth face. Lockwood, in a report to the Department of Justice, describes the multitude of risk factors that can contribute to violent behavior among youth: low school achievement or attachment to school; poor problem-solving skills; the reinforcement of aggressive behaviors through parenting behaviors; exposure to violence by media, in the community, or by peers; and a previous history of abuse or neglect.[8] Many at-risk youth also suffer from serious mental health problems, dealing with disorders such as posttraumatic stress, as well as mood and anxiety disorders. To think that we can prevent violent behavior without addressing these underlying causes is probably unrealistic.

Despite the serious limitations of zero-tolerance policies, we do not reject them entirely. In fact, we share many of their goals: sending a message to the school community that illegal and dangerous behaviors will not be tolerated, encouraging administrators to take decisive and predictable action rather than ignoring the behaviors, reducing aggressive acts, protecting the majority of students from a typically small group of dangerous youth, and improving learning environments for children. We, however, propose an alternative to no-choice expulsions, suspensions, and denial of children's educational opportunities. Our proposed alternatives do not compromise school safety and discipline. Yet the methods we advocate to reach these outcomes have an entirely different focus. Our efforts center on helping adolescents develop resiliency-supporting relationships. These relationships ultimately lead to a nonviolent school climate because they serve as a vehicle to address the school attachment, mental health, and educational issues of at-risk youth that when not addressed cause students to lash out.

We have learned from research showing that mentoring, or a supportive relationship with caring adults, is an effective strategy for fostering resiliency among at-risk youth.[9] In a review of evaluations of mentoring programs, Sipe reports that youth enrolled in Big Brothers/Big Sisters were 46 percent less likely than the control group to initiate drug use and were less likely to engage in physical conflicts.[10] Dryfoos writes, "The most significant feature common to . . . successful programs . . . was individual attention."[11] Similarly, Noguera writes that violence in schools often results because of a loss of connection and respect between teachers and students due to coercive structures that foster environments of mistrust and resistance. Feeling that they are being overly controlled, students often have such negative attitudes toward education that their school itself becomes a target of destruction and harassment.[12]

Research has also shown that academic performance in adolescent children is inversely correlated with antisocial behaviors such as aggression and substance abuse.[13] This means that as academic performance declines, students become more at risk for delinquent behaviors, and as risky behaviors increase, academic progress begins to deteriorate as well. Prevention and intervention must come not only from outside schools but also from within and must focus on eradicating the barriers that obstruct students' learning. Dryfoos notes that "poor school performance is both an antecedent and a consequence of substance abuse, teen parenthood, and various forms of delinquency."[14] McEvoy and Welker also explain that most current educational programs tend to treat conditions that affect academics as different from those that are associated with violence or aggression. They explain that the success of prevention programs is dependent on their ability to change the overall climate in which a student is immersed and the amount of time students spend with a caring adult.[15]

In this chapter, we introduce an approach to fostering academic success and emotional and mental health in the schools within a relational and developmental context. For the past seven years, we have built a framework and practice for at-risk youth, many with very serious psychological and social problems, who are struggling in the public school system. These types of students are also typically the recipients of the consequences of zero-tolerance policies. The program, RALLY (Responsive Advocacy for Life and Learning in Youth), has been implemented in two Boston schools and has entered the stage of a demonstration project with a number of replication sites underway across the country.

The RALLY approach

The RALLY program offers a fundamentally new way of providing support services to school children in order to increase academic achievement while addressing emotional and behavioral risks and challenges. The aim of this carefully evaluated program is to integrate the traditional distinctions between mental health and educational practice in work with at-risk children. Because educational excellence may act as a protective factor for at-risk youth, providing them with a sense of self-efficacy and tools for life success, RALLY interventions focus on supporting students' learning goals.

One response of school systems to the increasing behavioral and academic needs of students has been spending a large portion of their budgets referring these troubled or disruptive students to separate classrooms or to hospitals, residential schools, or diversion programs. Although these placements are important for some students, they are not appropriate for many. Youth may become increasingly stigmatized as special education students or patients, or criminalized and marked for their school careers as violent or oppositional. Recent research has also highlighted the problem of discriminatory practices whereby a disproportionate number of minority students are recommended for special education, suspension, and expulsion.[16]

Instead of relying on these typical pull-out services, the RALLY program advocates a "pull-in" model, whereby mental health clinicians, mentors, and youth workers bring their knowledge and practice to aid at-risk children in schools while supporting all children. We have found that this model works because it addresses the needs of students where many of their worlds intersect. Dryfoos, in a look at school-based social and health services, explains that schools must become more adept in dealing with a range of student needs, from addressing health concerns to resolving conflicts, because these high-risk behaviors have been shown to be interrelated with educational outcomes.[17] In contrast to traditional case management in which a child is pulled out of the classroom context to receive services, the RALLY model allows for services to be brought into the child's own environment, decreasing stigma and making these services available to all children.

RALLY goals

- To connect mental health and educational practice in work with "at-risk" children, focusing on removing the barriers to academic success.
- To place trained service providers *in the classroom with children*, improving support networks by "pulling services in" rather than "pulling children out."

- To expand children's schools into a hub for services, creating partnerships with neighborhood-based after-school programs, universities, health care and mental health providers.
- To actively bridge the different worlds of our students—home, neighborhood, school and after-school.
- To build test sites as a model for system-wide change.
- To continually assess and evaluate the program's effectiveness, while working collaboratively to put improvements into action.

A new professional role

At the center of the RALLY program is the prevention practitioner, a new professional role this program has developed.[18] These practitioners work to address the educational, mental health, and health needs of students and their families, whether students are considered at risk or not. These practitioners work both in and outside the classrooms at schools and focus on three primary objectives from a developmental point of view: relationship building and counseling, linking the different worlds of the child (school, home, peer, community), and providing academic support in classrooms. The model assumes that a prevention practitioner who provides the structure to bridge the child's experiences at school, at home, and in the community will greatly reduce the onset or continuation of problems by increasing school attachment and educational achievement.

The prevention practitioner works with all students in the class he or she has been assigned to support. Practitioners' activities include running groups, meeting with students individually, and providing in-classroom support. Practitioners assess students' risks and strengths in both academic and psychosocial functioning. They then use the relationships they build with students to facilitate the students' academic and personal growth. Individual and group meetings focus on improving academic performances and reducing the likelihood of participation in risky behaviors, such as drug use, delinquency, school failure, and school dropout. RALLY also works closely with teachers and school administrators to develop the program and to select and carefully tailor academic and recreational programs, both in and out of school. Practitioners meet with teachers and families to discuss how to work effectively with their challenged and challenging children within a three-tiered model of service delivery.

In Boston, the RALLY program trains practicum students from Harvard's Graduate School of Education to act as prevention practitioners under the supervision of McLean Hospital staff. In San Francisco, the Families on Track Program hires a full-time social work staff. In New York City, Fordham University students fill these roles. Practitioners could also be full-time school staff, behavior specialists, guidance counselors, social workers, or trained teachers. Most important is not who serves as practitioners but that they have the skills, training, and ongoing supervision they need to be effective in their roles. Many researchers have advocated for additional school personnel who are trained in violence prevention and are also able to address mental health concerns and early signs of high-risk behaviors.[19] These practitioners help to relieve the generally overburdened guidance counselors who have increasingly large caseloads and are often assigned noncounseling administrative duties.

RALLY introduces a new way of working in schools. By creating teams of practitioners and teachers working in classrooms to identify learning difficulties early on, we can intervene to teach children tools for success. By pulling services into the school and working with teachers to connect classroom lessons with personal growth, we demonstrate for children that learning affects all areas of their lives. We believe strongly that children, when guided by caring and knowledgeable adults, have tremendous resources to build their own strengths over time. RALLY's prevention program supports not only the national education goal to increase academic competency and to raise the standard of learning in the United States but also the goal of providing a safe school environment that is conducive to learning.[20] The RALLY program is not a "feel good" support program but is focused on helping children identify their strengths and areas of interest, as well as giving them a sense of belonging that will motivate them to attend school. Just as most parents and guardians strive to create a healthy balance between nurturing and limit setting at home, RALLY joins teachers and administrators who fight chaos and disruption by encouraging a set of consequences for dangerous behaviors while working to humanize our schools.

The three-tier model

Our model of connecting education, after-school learning, and mental health focuses on pulling in services to the classroom and the school, extending the context of treatment into the child's everyday experiences. This means that students who typically are pulled out of the classroom to receive academic, social, or psychological service now have similar services pulled into their classrooms. The goal is not only to intervene with students who have identifiable behavioral, academic, or social issues but also to prevent many of these problems from occurring in the first place. The traditional counseling model pulls children out of the classroom, further stigmatizing their behaviors and leaving the clinician without the important knowledge of the child's behavior outside the office. Clinicians typically lack firsthand knowledge of children's interactions with peers and other adults, making it more difficult for them to affect children's behavior and performance in the school setting. Clinicians in the school or community also generally do not see children until they are referred to them, meaning that students' ongoing problems frequently go unaddressed until they grow severe enough to warrant referral. We believe it is essential to use intervention funds for high-risk youth to benefit all children and teachers. In the process, those youth who are most in need of services are more likely to accept them due to lessened stigma and easier access, and all students benefit from the expert knowledge and relationship opportunities.

The RALLY program uses a three-tiered model of service delivery—high intensity (Tier One), targeted (Tier Two), and inclusive (Tier Three)—in order to serve all students and to help prevent problems before they affect children's academic performance and well-being (see Figure 6.1). Typically a coordinator arranges work in a cluster of classrooms, and practitioners work as a team with a teacher. The practitioner is not a teacher, a mental health counselor, or a tutor yet draws some skills from each of these roles. The practitioner spends full school days in a classroom to ensure continuity of work with teachers and students and a sufficient amount of face-to-face time with them. Although more time can be helpful, we have found that two days provide enough intensity that the practitioner can affect the climate of the classroom and be viewed as an important part of the students' (and teachers') lives.

High-intensity service delivery (Tier One)

The students with whom the practitioners work most closely are considered to be their high-intensity students, or part of Tier One. Because each classroom incorporates about five such students, we refer to this tier as the "High Fives," a way to keep the selection of children and the intervention as positive as possible. RALLY practitioners provide these students with weekly one-on-one tutoring and mentoring and interact regularly with their parents or guardians. These students, the primary focus of the practitioners' work, would traditionally be pulled out for services or would end up in residential settings or separate classrooms. Early in the school year, these students are identified with the help of teacher and practitioner observations, parent and guardian phone calls, students' requests, or indications from the students' previous school records. Tier One students represent a range of learning styles, socioeconomic backgrounds, and family histories, but all are selected because they are considered to be at risk for school violence or aggression, academic failure, truancy and dropout, depression and suicidality, gang involvement, social problems, early sexual activity, or substance use. Since risk factors and problems tend to travel in bundles, many of the high-intensity-tier students present a multitude of issues. Yet these "High Fives" do more than just ensure resources for themselves; they are the main reason that all children and their teachers receive support and expertise. Such students often view special services with suspicion and despair. RALLY

Figure 6.1. Three levels of prevention practice in the RALLY program

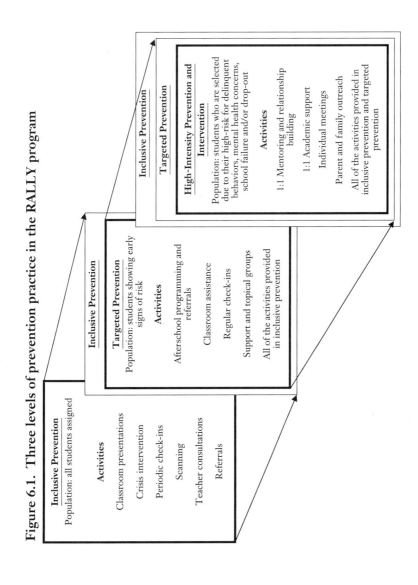

Inclusive Prevention
Population: all students assigned

Activities

Classroom presentations

Crisis intervention

Periodic check-ins

Scanning

Teacher consultations

Referrals

Inclusive Prevention

Targeted Prevention
Population: students showing early signs of risk

Activities

Afterschool programming and referrals

Classroom assistance

Regular check-ins

Support and topical groups

All of the activities provided in inclusive prevention

Inclusive Prevention

Targeted Prevention

High-Intensity Prevention and Intervention
Population: students who are selected due to their high-risk for delinquent behaviors, mental health concerns, school failure and/or drop-out

Activities

1:1 Mentoring and relationship building

1:1 Academic support

Individual meetings

Parent and family outreach

All of the activities provided in inclusive prevention and targeted prevention practitioners, however, are viewed by these students as positive additions to their school experience.

As middle school students, these youths are at an especially precarious position in the developmental process. Common to preadolescents, they are faced with increasing access to high-risk behaviors yet often experience less supervision and accountability.[21] In the transition from the elementary school single-classroom system to multiple classrooms with multiple teachers, students suddenly become responsible to several teachers, which can make it difficult for parents to establish relationships with each of their child's teachers and difficult for teachers to be accountable for each of their students. For students who enter middle school with negative attitudes toward education, poor educational and personal past experiences, or histories of school suspensions and disciplinary action, the likelihood is greatly increased that they will fail in this significant transition to middle school.

School-age children and adolescents face a cluster of factors that put them at risk for delinquent behaviors and correlated school failure. Developmentally, adolescents are highly influenced by their peers, and if they begin to evidence aggression and antisocial behavior, they often become part of a deviant clique of peers who constantly reinforce their oppositional behavior.[22] It then becomes increasingly difficult for these youth to step out of this role, especially if they are treated negatively by adults.

Considering all of the risk factors of these children, it is important to acknowledge their personal resiliency, because many children succeed despite overwhelming odds against them. Researchers have begun to identify protective factors such as caring adult relationships, support systems (school, home, neighborhood), and individual characteristics such as skills, easy temperament, and flexible social adaptation that act to reduce the effect of exposure to risk.[23] The RALLY program works to foster this resiliency through supportive relationships by building on students' strengths and helping them to grow developmentally and achieve large and small successes in academic and nonacademic work. Understanding that protective factors in a child's environment may decrease violent behavior, practitioners use multiple prevention strategies that are employed across systems (such as school, after school, and family) in order to be most effective. Decreasing aggression often requires a multidimensional approach because many children experience violence not solely in school but also in their neighborhoods, with the media, their peers, and their families.

Alan was a child on a downward spiral toward school dropout and delinquency. [In this example and others in this chapter, the names of students, teachers, parents, and practitioners have been changed to protect the identities of those involved.] He had already been assigned a parole officer and was fourteen years old and in the sixth grade by the second year that RALLY had been working with him. With support and guidance from the adults in his life, Alan was able to turn his second year in sixth grade into a positive experience instead of being constantly disruptive and fighting with his peers and teachers. Recent research has correlated grade retention with increased dropout rates and school failure and has shown that it is important for youth to understand that they can succeed even if they repeat a grade.[24]

Alan's mother requested that he be part of the RALLY program when he entered the school midyear. She was concerned that Alan had shown a great deal of anger and aggression while in elementary school and at his previous middle school, and as a result he had had a very hard time with his teachers and peers. He was often sent out of his classes, which resulted in numerous suspensions and missed days of school.

Alan's mother and his RALLY practitioner, Mr. D, set up a schedule of speaking once a month, with face-to-face meetings as necessary, making sure to talk whenever Alan was having a difficult time so that they could develop methods of supporting him at home and at school. Alan's mother contacted Mr. D for help again midway through the year, when the family moved in with relatives, leaving Alan with no personal space and nowhere to do his homework. To give him a place to do his work and to unwind, she enrolled him in RALLY's after-school program at Taft.

At the end of the year, Alan's mother told Mr. D that he had the best academic year of his life with the best grades, minimal fighting, and more happiness than she had ever seen. Although there had been so much improvement, Alan had entered the school with such low grades that he was unable to pass the standardized tests required for promotion.

It was a huge disappointment for Alan to repeat the sixth grade, but his new RALLY practitioner, Mr. S, began working with him early in the year to help ease the transition. Mr. S decided to focus on Alan's motivation and reasons for wanting to pass the sixth grade, as well as helping him with his academic work. Although there were ups and downs over the year, Alan's teachers remarked that he was trying much harder to hand in all of his schoolwork and was less of a distraction in the classroom. Mr. S also worked with Alan's mother to address ongoing attendance and behavioral concerns. In particular, one teacher who had been very vocal about how much of a problem Alan was in her classroom remarked in a cluster meeting that he was "turning himself around." At the end of the year, Alan passed all of his standardized tests and his courses and was promoted to seventh grade. He has been able to sustain his success and continue to use strategies other than aggression to deal with inevitable frustration at school.

With students like Alan, zero-tolerance rhetoric will never lead to the level of integrated services, supportive relationships, and educational supports necessary to these youths' success. While well-run schools often have student supports available, it was the practitioner's close collaboration with the teacher and the relationship with the student in the classroom, where aggression manifested itself, that created the basis of change. Engaging the mother to seek additional community help was also essential. This empowerment of parents by helping them access existing resources is an important aspect of RALLY. We do not believe we can solve all problems we encounter in schools. We can, however, orchestrate the integration of existing services, activities, and programs by a person whom the school, family, and child trust.

Adolescent boys and girls need a great deal of support to learn how to negotiate life and develop goals that are beneficial to them in the long run. It is useful to orient work with oppositional children toward the formation of joint goals, where the child has a sense of control and choice. RALLY tailors intervention strategies to students. Although the program is strongly steeped in a model of relationship building and resilience, psychoanalytic, Rogerian, and behavioral principals are applied whenever appropriate. But rather than forcing practitioners and children to fit theory, we tailor interventions to the students' developmental needs and accomplishments.[25]

Targeted intervention (Tier Two)

For students showing early signs of high-risk behavior, practitioners offer targeted interventions such as academic or support groups, crisis intervention, after-school programs, and referrals for health and mental health services. These students are considered part of Tier Two and are generally 30 to 50 percent of a practitioner's work with students. Much of the time, these students' needs are not identified right away but emerge during the school year as they begin to accept and trust this adult in their classroom. In addition, unexpected events can trigger crisis in otherwise well-adapted youth. For example, students have become homeless midyear; experiment with gang involvement; witness violence in their neighborhoods, home, or school; or suffer the loss of a parent, grandparent, or sibling. Many of these events are sufficiently problematic that students keep them a secret.

The fact that many students live in high-risk environments leads them to require identification, support, and intervention. Parental divorce, incarceration, and unemployment are only a few examples of the frequent adverse events that students are exposed to. These risk factors raise the probability that many youth who do well in the beginning of the year will show significant distress or even post-traumatic stress sometime during the school year. It is often the students who have adapted well in school and who react quietly to new stresses who are the ones who do not know how to ask for help and do not receive any services. This is especially unfortunate because problems that can be treated successfully with limited resources when addressed early on often lead to chronic (and expensive) disorders if allowed to fester. This early detection function, providing support at the time of first need, is enormously productive in our pull-in practice. We have observed too many schools and classrooms where the quiet suffering of traumatized children, unacknowledged depression, and even suicidality remain hidden. And yet it takes little to build trust so that students will confide and ask for help.

Despite the fact that some overt and aggressive behaviors can look very similar to those of the Tier One group, they need to be understood differently. A child without a history of aggression who has an outburst at school should typically not be the recipient of zero-tolerance treatment. To the contrary, the child should have consequences imposed on him or her in accordance with school guidelines, but should also be shown a great deal of tolerance and understanding to avoid a sense of victimization. School personnel and others will help to prevent further outbursts by focusing on the fact that the child has been able to avoid aggressive behaviors in the past and may have encountered new stresses. By building on these assets and the child's strengths instead of automatically expelling or suspending him or her, schools can work toward helping students change their behaviors and continue on a positive academic and developmental trajectory. To be sure, RALLY encourages and enforces consequences for aggressive behaviors that are tailored to the severity of the action—but always in the context of understanding the child's particular circumstances.

As many teachers and school staff have realized, youth violence often occurs between children who know one another, beginning with relatively minor incidents that quickly escalate into more serious behavior.[26] Along these lines, conflict resolution and mediation of conflicts by peers or adults become an important part of the targeted services offered to students. In middle school especially, students often get into finger pointing that can be easily diffused, but if left to simmer can quickly evolve into larger problems. Van Acker and Talbott write that many middle school children lack the necessary social skills to solve common problems.[27] When they are punished for these inappropriate behaviors (for example, slapping a classmate who laughs at a test grade), they miss out on the opportunity to acquire new behaviors, and they may build resistance against an autocratic disciplinary system. Practitioners often have the necessary time to intervene and take advantage of the many conflicts that arise, to enhance problem-solving skills and negotiation strategies.

In our experience, these problems often arise not only with high-risk youth but also with students at Tier Two or Three as well, which is why it is essential to get to know all of the children. Only then can practitioners intervene early in conflicts, reducing the overall violence in schools. The next example is of a child who did not fit into the high-risk group yet needed significant support during the school year.

Marissa identified herself to her practitioner, Ms. J, early in the year, asking to talk to her about other girls in her class. She had difficulty making friends and often took Mrs. J aside to tell her that she was "going to fight this girl." She became part of Mrs. J's girls' group, which focused on building friendships and resolving conflicts. The group met weekly, and Marissa was one of the more vocal members. She especially enjoyed telling the other girls how she had gotten into fights in elementary school and in her neighborhood. Her solution to all conflicts was to "fight it out." The majority of her time and energy was devoted to conflict with others, and thus her academic work suffered to the point that she needed to repeat the grade.

In contrast to her past reputation, she entered her second year in sixth grade with a new set of goals, which included better behavior in class and a more serious attitude toward her school work. Her new attitude and effort showed in her improved classroom and homework performance. But the most significant change was how she dealt with conflict. When a classmate began to spread rumors about Marissa and threatened her safety, she went directly to her new teachers and her practitioner. Marissa asked if a meeting could be set up between her and the other student to resolve the issue. This was made possible and led to a successful end of a potentially dangerous situation. Marissa had learned how to ask for help and how to discuss conflict rather than engage in physical fights.

This example highlights another important point. The presence of practitioners in classrooms and their close working relationship with teachers leads students to have more open relationships with their teachers as well. This is a very important goal of RALLY, as we want to avoid a split between authority-oriented teachers and supportive practitioners.

Conflicts may also arise between teachers and students, and a RALLY practitioner can be instrumental in helping students learn to explain themselves and their actions in less confrontational ways. Practitioners may also help teachers recognize students who are motivated to change their behavior and work to mediate disagreements.

One day during lunch, Mrs. C brought Douglas down to the RALLY office looking very distraught. She told Ms. L, Douglas's prevention practitioner, "He's upset with me, and I don't know why—but I thought he should talk to you, because he doesn't want to talk to me right now." She explained that he had been refusing to look at her or talk to her for the second half of the class period, no matter how hard she tried to get his attention. Since he was generally a well-behaved student, she was particularly frustrated and confused by his actions.

Mrs. C had let Ms. L know earlier that week, in front of Douglas, that his grades were slipping and that she was trying to address the problem with him. Before Mrs. C left the room on the day she brought Douglas to see Ms. L; she explained to him that she really liked him and knew how smart he was, but she also knew he was not working at his potential.

After Mrs. C left, Douglas told Ms. L that Mrs. C was always picking on him and that he did not deserve this treatment. "Other kids do worse stuff than me, and she doesn't criticize them. She's just doing it to be mean, and she's nagging!" They discussed the teacher's intentions (to enhance his academic success) and her method of communication, which was adverse to him. Next, Ms. L and Douglas role-played a discussion with Mrs. C, in which he told her that he was interpreting her behavior as nagging and that it upset him. The three of them—teacher, practitioner, and student—then met, and he explained to Mrs. C why he was so angry with her. She explained that she was only "nagging" because she cared and that she would be more conscious of her words in the future. They decided that he could give her a thumbs-up or thumbs-down sign at the end of the period to let her know how he was feeling and that he in turn would be less negative in class. Although this intervention did not lead to immediate and total success, it provided the student with a voice and a possibility of reconnecting to the teacher instead of engaging in an unproductive struggle of wills.

Students with learning problems or who may just be struggling with the academic workload can often express their frustration by acting out in class. If these concerns are not given the proper attention, the students often become overwhelmed with the demands from their environment and express their frustration and lack of impulse control with aggression or violence. In zero-tolerance environments, they tend to be pushed out of the classroom and the school, accelerating their rage and frustration. Whenever possible, school personnel should go to the source of the acting-out behavior and intervene before the escalation occurs.

Practitioners also spend a great deal of time in classrooms, where they are able to scan for students who look sad or withdrawn, whose affect has changed dramatically, or who are having difficulty paying attention or sitting still. The practitioners are trained and supervised to work with these students, but when situations persist, they may be referred for evaluations or outside counseling. This referral process is made much easier for students by already having a relationship with their RALLY practitioner. Adolescents and their families do not typically feel comfortable going to unknown outside providers, and we have found that a person whom they trust and who can go with them, or help to create that bridge, can be essential to success. Once this bridge is established, the practitioner also tries to bring back information for the teachers and the school about medication and other relevant information. It is essential to be clear about confidentiality and privacy issues. However, if the school is to make appropriate accommodations, some flow of information is necessary. Most schools have a system in place to deal with outside providers, but we have found the area of communication between teachers and external services to be very lacking.

In the middle of the year, Wally, a twelve-year-old Hispanic student, was constantly disrupting his class, calling out to his friends and interrupting his teacher. His RALLY practitioner, Ms. O, observed him in various contexts (math class, gym, after school) and began to meet individually with him. His mother shared with Ms. O that he had acted like this off and on for years and that he had been kicked out of school on numerous occasions because of his lack of self-control. Ms. O spent time building a relationship with Wally's mother, explaining sources of attention problems, and working with her to set up an evaluation for attention deficit hyperactivity disorder (ADHD) through his pediatrician. She also gathered

ADHD scales and observations from his teachers to pass on to his doctor. Wally was eventually diagnosed with ADHD and started on medication. During this time, RALLY kept in close contact with his doctors and his mother while the medication was being regulated. Many adjustments were made until a dosage was found that allowed Wally to stay focused throughout the day with minimal side effects. Ms. O was also able to work with Wally's teachers to support him in the classroom as he made the transition to a more active student and participant in learning. Although his grades and behavior improved, the progress was slow. His mother worked with his teachers and RALLY staff to use techniques at home that would make it easier for him to complete his homework and study for tests. With this added support, Wally was finally able to experience some success in the classroom, and his attitude toward school became much more positive.

Groups are also a particularly effective method for helping students work together and connect outside class around emotional, academic, or social issues. A significant part of the support offered by RALLY to Tier Two students occurs in group settings. Groups may be formed to address specific issues that students are concerned about, including managing anger, developing social skills, learning how to resolve conflicts, cultivating leadership skills, dealing with the loss of loved ones, or acquiring organizational skills. Often practitioners also run academic groups to help students who are experiencing similar academic difficulties, while capitalizing on their needs for social interaction and development. These groups offer a much-needed chance for students to practice their social skills and learn to problem-solve with the guidance of a trained and caring adult who works to facilitate positive interactions. The academic focus of many of these groups underscores how RALLY is not a traditional mental health intervention but a program that sees its mission in schools as focusing on children's learning and academic success.

Inclusive (Tier Three)

The inclusive tier consists of the entire classroom, generating intervention for all students. The practitioner does brief monthly or bimonthly check-ins with each student, allowing them time to talk about their interests, achievements, and concerns. The effects from these short meetings can be very powerful, and the fact that all students participate in these meetings prevents any child from feeling singled out.

Teachers and practitioners also collaborate to plan classroom presentations and design ways the practitioner can work within the classroom to support students academically. Instead of outside agencies' bringing in visiting curricula, practitioners have the opportunity to use their inside knowledge of the students in their classrooms to tailor projects and presentations. Each RALLY practitioner works within classrooms in different ways, depending on the teacher's preference, the practitioner's own interests, the type of classroom environment, and the subject being taught.

One prevention practitioner, Ms J, used adventure-based learning as an opportunity to work with all of the students in her assigned homerooms. She worked out a schedule with her pair teacher where she took one class period every two weeks to run self-confidence and team-building workshops with both of her classes.

This interaction worked on many levels because it created situations where students could problem-solve and get to know each other. Students who were quiet in class had a chance to express themselves, and students who had difficulty with academic subjects were able to shine. The activities ranged from things like "The Human Knot" and "Role-Model Skits" to more difficult adventure challenges like "The Modified Spider Web" and "Peanut-Butter Meltdown." In one simple activity, the class tried to get a hula-hoop to reach the floor while keeping the hula-hoop completely parallel to the ground. It was an exercise in communication, patience, strategy, and teamwork, and they all got to participate in a hula-hoop contest when they met their goal.

Mejia, a student who was generally very impulsive and had difficulties following directions for academic work, was able to excel in this setting. Although he had a reputation as a fighter, over time he was able to change that into a reputation as a leader as he was able to lead the group in decision-making activities in the classroom.

This kind of team-oriented programming allows all students to have significant involvement in the RALLY program and keeps the Tier One students with whom practitioners work more intensively from being stigmatized. As a prevention practitioner, Mrs. Jules felt that she truly became accessible and effective to all the students in her classes. We have institutionalized this experiential learning in a joint program between RALLY, the YMCA in Boston's Allston-Brighton area, and the Taft Middle School. All sixth graders, their teachers, and the practitioners engage in team-building activities as they begin their school year and their careers in middle school. RALLY, the YMCA, and the teachers continue this training at the school throughout the year. As research has shown, when schools can work to affect the overall atmosphere in the classrooms by using engaging instruction, schoolwide initiatives that promote prosocial behavior, and positive classroom management techniques, they help to buffer the risk factors that youth face in school.[28] Practitioners may also work with teachers to consult on students' particular learning styles and help them accommodate challenging students. The next example illustrates a practitioner and teacher working together to find a solution for a child's lack of motivation.

One of the RALLY prevention practitioner's main goals with the inclusive tier is to connect students to activities and services in their community. Practitioners are able to distribute information about opportunities for students and families and then follow up with specific students. After getting to know each student, practitioners work to match children's strengths and interests with opportunities in their neighborhoods. Practitioners focus on strengthening ties between the students' in-school and after-school lives, helping students work on their learning goals, and giving students time to explore nonacademic strengths.

Many students involved in the RALLY program are referred to after-school programs, tutoring, mental health services, summer camps, mentoring programs, and sports teams. Practitioners may direct children to activities that foster confidence, identify and strengthen unique talents, encourage future goal development, or support academic growth. Much of the RALLY coordinator's time is spent finding programs that are a good fit for the students, building on the resources and institutional collaboration that past coordinators have established. Effort is spent visiting programs with students and families, calling parents, and following through with the program to ensure connection is made between the school and the community programs with which the student is involved. We have found that trying to connect students with organizations by mail or by putting up posters in hallways does not work. Students go to programs and access services more often when they are actively encouraged and personally connected through a friend or an adult. RALLY practitioners work to fulfill this bridging function. Students do not have to be in Tier One or Two in order to benefit from high-quality out-of-school programming.

Research has shown that students who participate in after-school programs often have significantly better grades in reading and math than their peers do.[29] These students also may show improvements in behavior and attendance and a reduction of risky behaviors such as substance use, early sexual activity, and juvenile crime. Practitioners are essential links in this effort to form a net of prevention around children by linking organizations that provide after-school activities with families and school systems. RALLY works on both the personal level of inserting practitioners into schools and the institutional level of helping create a network of collaborating organizations serving children and families.

Keysha tried out for the RALLY-initiated girls' soccer team early in the spring semester of the school year. She had struggled all year to make friends, to stand up to bullying and teasing from boys in her classroom, and to control her temper. The boys in the classroom often singled Keysha out because she was much taller and larger than many of the other girls, and they often made hurtful comments to her behind the teacher's back. When she began playing soccer, the students discovered that her size was an asset on the playing field and that she was a star defense player.

With this newfound confidence from playing soccer and with the support of her teammates, coaches, and practitioners, Keysha was now better able to respond to teasing. Before, she had responded with physical force and angry outbursts directed at her classmates, teachers, or anyone else around her; now, she was better able to channel her frustration. Keysha and her prevention practitioner pointed this out to her homeroom teacher, who was able to recognize and work with her to address the problem of bullying and teasing in the classroom.

Conclusion

When we began RALLY, we had a strong sense of the scope of the problems facing schools, families, and communities. We also recognized that the traditional separation of educational, health, and community resources could not respond appropriately to the crisis in education and mental health, nor could it stem the tide of the increasing hazards facing our youth. Thus, we embarked on an exploration of integrating services in a fundamentally different way by defining a new professional role and seeking partners in our efforts.[30] It has not always been easy; we needed to remain flexible and have teachers and administrators help us define this new role, but they, along with students, have become our greatest allies. Teachers and administrators have been overwhelmingly positive and supportive of this program due in part to the ways in which we are able to address children's academics and behaviors across settings and effect change.

Teachers and students can work better together when added supports are in place. The effectiveness of our program has led us to work to change traditional views of mental health and education and to work to convince policymakers to push for larger changes. We cannot expect teachers to serve as mental health practitioners, family and community outreach workers, and mentors in today's environment of increased risk factors without seriously compromising their own quality of life or the quality of their students' education. Schools are in need of many services and are expected not only to raise test scores but also to make sure that children are ready to learn and are socially, emotionally, and mentally fit. We believe that schools, after-school programs, and community services can be better integrated in order to prevent the very behaviors that zero tolerance attempts to eradicate.

As most nonprofit agencies and new programs know, programs must be cost-effective and practical if they are to survive. The costs of a program such as RALLY are significant, but the alternatives are far more expensive. If a prevention practitioner can help avoid placing only one or two children in a more restrictive classroom setting or residential school, they have saved school systems enough money to pay for the intervention and prevention work of an entire cluster of classrooms. This calculation does not include the savings to society for detecting and treating problems early, thus avoiding chronicity of disorders or incarceration. Increased academic success also pays for itself many-fold.

Unfortunately, these calculations alone will not easily produce necessary resources in schools, so RALLY is concentrating on the following avenues to implement the activities beyond its demonstration sites:

- Increasing mental health spending in schools and delivering services not only in school clinics but also around a three-tiered model using the classroom as a center of intervention and prevention.
- Supporting the creation of prevention and community coordinators for every school who can help create the bridging of services and activities at the interface of schools, families, and communities. These coordinators represent an important first step for schools that cannot afford practitioners in classrooms.
- Providing guidance to universities that can make a contribution by encouraging and supervising students who can take on RALLY functions in schools.
- Working with the growing after-school movement to train qualified youth workers to join part of the school day, thus working to link students' in-school and out-of-school time.

What we are learning at our demonstration sites can help guide these four ways of increasing RALLY roles in many schools and classrooms around the country. Our work establishing this new practice and role, as well as the training that is required, represents a productive and realistic alternative to discipline policies such as zero tolerance. When schools become places where students want to learn instead of institutions where children and teachers feel estranged and families and communities are marginalized, then the overall safety and quality of education will increase.

As youth violence continues to be a problem in many schools, administrators, parents, and government agencies will search for effective ways to decrease delinquent and aggressive behaviors within school walls. One answer has been the zero-tolerance policies, which have not been shown to be particularly effective and may actually be harmful to the development of children. If we can connect the worlds of children and focus on the early detection of educational, social, and mental health issues, we will affect some of the root causes that lead to the very behaviors that zero tolerance wants to curb. Lasting solutions require transforming what does not work for students, administrators, teachers, and parents. No rhetoric of quick fixes will ever bring about these urgently needed changes.[31]

Notes

1. American Bar Association. (2001). *Zero tolerance report.* Available: www.abanet.org/crimjust/juvjus/zerotolreport.html.

2. Curwin, R., & Mendler, A. (1999). Zero tolerance for zero tolerance. *Phi Beta Kappan, 81*(2), 119–120; Noguera, P. (1995). Preventing and producing violence: A critical analysis of responses to school violence. *Harvard Educational Review, 65*(2), 189–212; Skiba, R., & Peterson, R. (1999, January). The dark side of zero tolerance: Can punishment lead to safe schools? *Phi Beta Kappan,* pp. 1–4; Van Acker, R., & Talbott, E. (1999). The school context and risk for aggression: Implications for school-based prevention and intervention efforts. *Preventing School Failure, 44*(1), 12–19.

3. Harvard Civil Rights Project. (2000). *Opportunities suspended: The devastating consequences of zero tolerance and school discipline policies.* Cambridge, MA: Author. p. 3. Available: www.law.harvard.edu/group/civilrights/conferences/zero/zt.html.

4. Skiba & Peterson. (1999).

5. Furlong, M., & Morrison, G. (2000). The school in school violence. *Journal of Emotional and Behavioral Disorders, 8*(3), 71–82.

6. Eccles, J. S. (1999). The development of children ages 6 to 14. *The Future of Children: When School Is Out, 9,* 30–44.

7. Editorial. (2000, June 9). *Chicago Tribune.*

8. Lockwood, D. (1997). *Violence among middle school and high school students: An analysis and implications for prevention.* Washington, DC: U.S. Department of Justice, Office of Justice Programs, National Institute of Justice.

9. Dryfoos, J. (1991). School-based social and health services for at-risk students. *Urban Education, 26*(1), 118–137; Masten, A. (1994). Resilience in individual development: Successful adaptature, and school climate: A critical review. *Journal of Emotional and Behavioral Disorders, 8*(3), 130–140; Noam, G., Winner K., Rhein, A., & Molad, B. (1996). The Harvard RALLY Program and the prevention practitioner: Comprehensive, school-based intervention to support resiliency in at-risk adolescents. *Journal of Child and Youth Care Work, 11*, 32–47.

10. Sipe, C. L. (1999). Mentoring adolescents: What have we learned? In J. B. Grossman (Ed.), *Contemporary issues in mentoring.* Philadelphia: Public/Private Venture.

11. Dryfoos. (1991).

12. Noguera. (1995). p. 124.

13. Dryfoos, J. (1990). *Adolescents-at-risk: Prevalence and prevention.* New York: Oxford University Press; Lockwood. (1997). McEvoy, A., & Welker, R. (2000). Antisocial behavior, academic failure, and school climate: A critical review. *Journal of Emotional and Behavioral Disorders, 8*, 130–140.

14. Dryfoos. (1991). p. 122.

15. McEvoy & Welker. (2000).

16. Harvard Civil Rights Project. (2000). Skiba & Peterson. (1999).

17. Dryfoos. (1991).

18. Noam et al. (1996).

19. Cunningham, N., & Sandhu, D. (2000). A comprehensive approach to school-community violence prevention. *Professional School Counseling, 4*(2), 126–133; Dryfoos. (1991).

20. National Educational Goals Panel. (2000). *Goal #7. Safe, disciplined, and alcohol- and drug-free schools.* Washington, DC: Author.

21. Shirley, D. (1997). *Community organizing for school reform.* Austin, TX: University of Texas.

22. Henry, D. (2000). Peer groups, families and school failure among urban children: Elements of risk and successful interventions. *Preventing School Failure, 44*(3), 97–104.

23. Hawkins, J. D., Arthur, M. W., & Catalano, R. F. (1995). Preventing substance abuse. In M. Tonry & D. Farrington (Eds.), *Building a safer society: Strategic approaches to crime prevention* (pp. 124–186). Chicago: University of Chicago Press.

24. Hauser, R., Simmons, S., & Pager, D. (2001, January 13). *Trends in high school dropout among white, black, and Hispanic youth, 1972–1998.* Paper presented at Dropouts in America conference sponsored by Project ACHIEVE and the Civil Rights Project at Harvard University.

25. Noam, G., Pucci, K., & Foster, E. (1999). Development, resilience and school success in youth. In D. Cicchetti & S. Toth (Eds.), *Developmental psychopathology: Developmental approaches to prevention and intervention.* Rochester,

NY: University of Rochester Press.
  26. Lockwood, D. (1997).
  27. Van Acker & Talbott. (1999).
  28. Shulman, H. (1996). Using developmental principles in violence prevention. *Elementary School Guidance and Counseling, 30*(1), 170–180.
  29. National Institute on Out-of-School Time. (1997), *Fact sheet on school-age children's out-of-school-time.* Wellesley, MA: Wellesley College, 1997.
  30. We would like to thank the following organizations for their generous support of RALLY's work: The Alden Trust, FleetBoston Bank, The Klingenstein Third Generation Foundation, The Leon Lowenstein Foundation, Partners' Community Benefits Department, and Roche Relief Fund of the U.S. Trust Company.
  31. We would like to acknowledge the editorial assistance and excellent comments of Cheri Goldstein.

GIL G. NOAM, the director and founder of the RALLY program and the program in After-School Education and Research, is associate professor of psychiatry/psychology at McLean Hospital and Harvard Medical School and associate professor of education at the Harvard Graduate School of Education, Cambridge, Massachusetts.

LAURA A. WARNER is the coordinator of the RALLY demonstration site at the W. H. Taft Middle School in Allston-Brighton, Massachusetts.

LEIGH VAN DYKEN is the associate program director of RALLY and is also in charge of training, consultation, and technical assistance for new programs.

Index